SECRETS

FOR

SUCCESSFUL

SEARCHING

Professional secrets of how to find almost anyone!

by Norma Tillman
Private Investigator

© 1992 Norma Tillman, U.F.O., Inc.

U.F.O., Inc.
P.O. Box 290333
Nashville, TN 37229-0333

All rights reserved.

No part of this book may be reproduced or transmitted in any form or by any means, electronic or mechanical, including photocopying, recording or by any information retrieval system, without the written permission of the author/publisher, expect where permitted by law.

Some of the graphics used in this publication are products from Presentation Task Force, CGM V4.0 Presentation Task Force is a registered trademark of New Vision Technologies, Inc.

Editors: Vicki, Terri and Lisa

ISBN 0-9634424-0-6

Library of Congress 92-061680

PREFACE

Anyone interested in finding someone needs this book. People search for others for many reasons. Some get lost in the shuffle of life. Others may be hiding. Hiding from child support payments, from alimony payments, or perhaps just dropping out from life. There are many adoptees seeking birth parents and many birth parents seeking the children they gave up for adoption. Private investigators, attorneys, paralegals, bondsmen, insurance adjustors, police officers, relatives seeking lost relatives, skip tracers, all can benefit from this book.

Step by step use of public records, the location of the records, and how to use those records are outlined. Samples of needed forms are also included. Available commercial databases which can be used for searching, are described.

The necessary information to get started searching, as well as where to start and how to search are described.

From the Author

Over the years I have found hundreds of missing persons. Usually they were no further away than the telephone. The techniques I used to find these people can be used by ordinary people, i.e. those interested in genealogy, police officers, private investigators, attorneys, paralegals, collection agencies, bondsmen, landlords, etc., using the records of our very own government.

I have experienced tremendous personal satisfaction finding and uniting missing persons with relatives and loved ones. I have also experienced personal satisfaction finding debtors who have skipped out, those refusing to pay child support and so on. All of these persons I have found using very simple methods. I just looked them up in our government's records.

After 18 years searching these records, it has become apparent to me that this skill can be used by anyone. I think of it as a game. To play the game, you must know the rules, the other players, and you must know what it takes to win. These secrets are shared with you in this book.

Do not feel that every missing person may be located using these methods. I have found that the great majority can be located. However, there are rare exceptions. Your chances for success are greatly enhanced using these methods, but there are no guarantees.

I believe one of the reasons I have been so successful at locating missing persons and finding other information is because of my attitude, patience and mannerism. In other words, I treat people nicely, with respect and understanding. As a result, people are nice to me.

The examples used in this book are from actual cases I have worked. The names are changed to respect the privacy of those concerned.

Table of Contents

Chapter I	Methodology	1
Chapter II	Court Systems	9
Chapter III	Records	15
	A. Directories	16
	B. Local	20
	C. Court	27
	D. State	35
	E. Federal	57
	F. Other	75
	G. Utilities	78
	H. Last Known Address	79
Chapter IV	Searching	83
Chapter V	The Privacy Act	87
Chapter VI	The Freedom of Information Act (FOIA)	89
Chapter VII	A Comparison of the Privacy Act and The Freedom of Information Act (FOIA)	91
Chapter VIII	Credit Card Companies	93
Chapter IX	Fair Credit Reporting Act	95
Chapter X	Where To Write For Records	111
Chapter XI	Genealogical Records	121
Chapter XII	Legal Adoption Process	139

Appendixes

Appendix A	Sample Missing Person Profile	165
Appendix B	Sample Missing Person Motive Profile	169
Appendix C	Sample Criminal History Record Check Request	171
Appendix D	Checklist for Searchers	173
Appendix E	Medical Authorization	177

FORWARD

Locating a missing person has never been easier. It is almost impossible for anyone living in the U.S. to exist without leaving some kind of record somewhere! Searchers have information available at their fingertips. Modern technology has made the searcher's job easier through the use of computer data bases. Without leaving the office or home, it is possible to obtain information within minutes with the right databases. Everyone, with the possible exception of those persons who have deliberately chosen to hide themselves, is on paper or in a computer somewhere! Every imaginable public record is available through the computer from driver's license, vehicle registration, divorce, marriage, birth and death records, bankruptcies, credit reports, liens and judgments. Most of us exist in computer and other records in many, many places. **THESE RECORDS MAY LEGALLY BE USED TO FIND PRACTICALLY ANYONE!** Sometimes it is only a matter of minutes before a person may be found through a Social Security Number or a last known address. Even telephone searches may only take minutes. A world of information is available at your fingertips. *If you need to locate a missing person this book is a must.*

The intent of this book is to explain the content of these records, and how to use them to find a missing person whether that person be a lost relative, adoptee, or even a criminal. You will also learn how and where to get credit information for lawful business purposes. Once you have finished reading this book you will be able to execute a public record search and retrieve relevant documents. The records listed herein are public and paid for with your tax dollars. You are entitled to use these records subject only to existing privacy laws. Your success is limited only by your imagination and the amount of information you can collect to begin the search.

It is not the intent of this book to train investigators, private or public. You need not be a professional investigator or law enforcement officer to learn these techniques. No license is necessary to research public records, however a license may be required if you receive payment for your services. Anyone who can read and write can learn to successfully use public records to find almost anyone who has not deliberately chosen to hide. In order to play the "search game", one must first understand how the records "system" works. In order to understand the records "system", one needs to be familiar with where records are kept. Once you understand what records are available, where they are kept and what you need to do to access them, you are ready to play.

Records may be in a public library, a state library, a court house, a city hall, a state office building or a federal office building. Included is a chapter on court systems because of the importance of court records. Courts are a veritable treasure chest of extremely accurate information filed in an easily retrievable manner.

A good searcher must have diligence, patience, determination, resourcefulness, creativity, understanding, knowledge and experience. Think of the search as working a jigsaw puzzle in which each piece of information helps make the complete picture or perhaps a treasure hunt with the information or missing person being the "pot of gold".

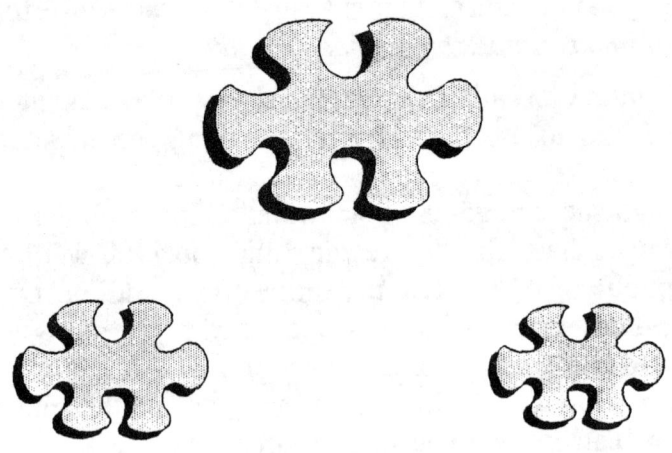

CHAPTER I - METHODOLOGY

Most missing persons can usually be located through the use of information contained in existing public and private records. The objective is to use this information to find the current location of the person being sought.

Although these records have always been available, searchers rarely have the skills to use them effectively when searching for missing persons. Believe it or not, most missing persons are not missing at all. In fact, marriage, divorce, illness, change of jobs, etc., leave paper trails which can be easily followed. It is impossible to live in our modern society without leaving a paper trail unless deliberate attempts are taken to avoid them. Changing identity is possible but difficult to maintain over time. Even changed identity can be cross checked for accuracy given sufficient time and reason. Learning to use these records is a skill which anyone can easily develop.

Paper trails are everywhere. Records with government, utility, bank, credit, insurance and medical history are some but not all records available to the investigator. Modern technology has provided easier access and cross checking, and promises to make efforts even easier in the future as records keepers take advantage of ever improving technology. The information available through these records is tremendous. Without leaving the office, computer checks may be made for driver's license, vehicle registration, marriage, divorce, bankruptcy, credit, forwarding address, employer, and a world of other information. It is possible to check all states and some foreign countries. The techniques and methods outlined here apply to those missing persons who are not deliberately hiding themselves from discovery. For whatever reason there are those who choose to hide themselves. The techniques for finding such persons are not the subject of this book.

In order to make full use of these records, it is necessary for the searcher to know and understand what these records are, where they are located, what information is contained in them, and where the information may lead. The searcher must make every effort to learn all that is possible to know about these records. The information provided herein will permit the reader to penetrate the bureaucracies of the city, county, state, and federal agencies, courts and other regulating bodies.

The methodology for searching for a missing person using existing records is simple. Follow these steps:

1. Assemble all known information.
2. Determine the start point.
3. Follow the trail in the records.

ASSEMBLE INFORMATION

The act of finding a missing person requires a starting point. That starting point is the assembling of all known information on the missing person into one file. The very best information to start with is the full name, date of birth, and social security number. With this information the searcher should be able to locate the missing person. If this information is not available, then whatever information the searcher has will provide the starting point. Essentially the starting point tells the searcher what record(s) to check first. Assemble all of the information provided by the person initiating the search and make sure to include the following if available:

- Last known address of the missing person.
- The telephone and address book of the missing person.
- Any correspondence or other personal records or files such as old rent receipts, credit card receipts, church or social affiliations, tax records, professional designations such as Real Estate Broker, etc. maintained by the missing person.
- A list of all known friends and relatives.

You will almost always start your search with the telephone. Whenever possible, obtain the Date of Birth (D.O.B.), Social Security Number (SSN), Driver's License Number (DL), Last Known Address (LKA), any telephone numbers, and the names or addresses and telephone numbers of friends or associates. If the subject had, or has, a professional designation such as Real Estate Broker, Insurance Agent, Commercial Driver, etc., obtain that information too. The quality of the information initially obtained will probably influence the outcome of the search with regard to time, effort and success.

Most public records may be accessed over the telephone. Either the information will be provided directly or the record agency will furnish instructions specifying the manner in which the records and their information may be accessed. So, the more information obtained from records, the greater the chance for success.

You will find it convenient to have pre-printed information forms, such as a checklist, a request for criminal history or a medical authorization form available for use in recording the initial information gathered for later transfer to your database. The information collected must be accurate. Keep in mind that some or all of the information assembled may be incorrect or deliberately misleading. Continue to check the accuracy and veracity of the information as your search progresses. Samples of these forms are included in Appendices D & E.

Chapter II describes the court systems and outlines which courts have what records. Many persons are hesitant to approach the county courthouse but should not be. You will find court staffs courteous and helpful.

Chapter III provides information on various records, where they are found, what they contain, and how they may be used to search or gain leads to search other less obvious records.

The examples listed are actual cases. These successful cases will demonstrate how missing persons are located using the paper trail. The examples will add to your expertise as you read through this book.

DETERMINE THE START POINT

The searcher needs useable and traceable information. Motive helps sort the useable information from the non-useable information. If reasons can be established for the disappearance of the missing person, it will be much easier to determine what records to start with first. Sometimes the information used to start with may not be altogether accurate or complete. This could be deliberate. It is up to the searcher to make this determination. Sometimes this realization will not occur until well into the search. Once this determination has been made it will provide a greater degree of confidence in the reliability of the information, therefore leading to a greater chance for success. A sample motive form is provided at Appendix B.

Sometimes the searcher will have more information than can be appropriately used. Time and experience will provide the searcher with the tools to decide what is useable and what is not.

When searching a paper trial, knowledge of characteristics of the missing person may often dictate which record to search first.

Personality and personal characteristics do not normally change. One will continue to have the same interests and enjoyments, hobbies and hangouts, and recreation when relocated from place to place. Fishermen will still fish and gamblers will still gamble. One may not frequent the same hangouts but will frequent the same type of hangouts. In other words, a person may change location but not personality and characteristics.

Once the initial information on the missing person is obtained, review it. The place to start will be obvious.

1. Usually, but not always, telephone and crisscross (reverse telephone directories are the first records used (the start point). These publications provide addresses, neighbors, and phone numbers. Neighbors may provide more unanticipated information.

2. Then vehicle and driver's license information and history may be used.

3. Then use property tax and real estate information.

4. Try to obtain a SSN.

5. Then traffic offenses or criminal proceedings.

6. If none of these are available then try marriage licenses, divorce records or civil process (lawsuits, judgments, liens).

7. Then use professional designations or military service.

Keep considering all possibilities until a record is found that will provide information on the missing person or direct you to another record where information may lead you to the missing person. Somewhere there is a record on the person sought. It is up to you to develop the skill and experience that will lead to success. Do not become discouraged. If Plan A does not work, there is always Plan B, C, D and E.

FOLLOW THE TRAIL IN THE RECORDS

Information in the records will lead to addresses and/or phone numbers which can lead to additional addresses, friends, phone numbers, places of employment and so on. License numbers lead to addresses, accident reports, and other vehicles. Registration and/or accident reports may lead not only to insurance companies, but perhaps also to a tow truck, ambulance, hospital, bondsman, or police officer which may result in an address or phone number. Information in one type of record may lead to another record which may result in a current address or employer. If the current address is not available through one record, it is available in another, perhaps in another city, county, or state. Remember, the object of the search is to determine the current location of the missing person. Following a paper trail may be compared to working a puzzle. Each piece of information acquired will help to reach the objective. Keep the information organized in a file in an easily retrievable manner.

The file should contain:
- The missing person profile.
- The missing person motive profile.
- Names, addresses and phone numbers of all persons contacted.
- Agencies and associated records researched with contact names and phone numbers.
- Copies of records and related documents.
- Summaries of conversations of all persons contacted.
- All other information.
- Ensure that all information is in one file.

It is important to remember to be prepared to pay a fee for information and or copies. Most jurisdictions now charge small fees to help cover the cost of their operations.

IMPOSSIBLE TRAILS TO FOLLOW

Not every missing person can be traced as you well know. It is virtually impossible to track someone without a paper trail. There are many circumstances in which a paper trail may not be available, such as:
- Subject may be institutionalized. Approximately two and one-half million Americans are in prison, nursing homes, mental hospitals, or other facility.
- Subject may be living in another country.
- Subject may be deceased. (Death records are available through the Social Security Death Index. A master file of all deaths since 1962 is available by name only through certain databases. Mormon church libraries have death records available for persons working on genealogies. Archive libraries and public libraries have census records.

- Subject may be using a false identity by assuming the identity of a deceased person, using stolen identification, or even by being protected by the government in a witness protection program.
- Subject may be protected by an underground movement, such as a group providing safe houses for persons who take children in child custody suits in which sexual abuse of the child is involved. Motorcycle gangs have long provided safe houses to members who are wanted by law-enforcement.
- Subject may be a member of a cult or commune cut off from worldly association.
- Subject may be hiding from law-enforcement and will go to great lengths to be constantly moving often from place to place. By staying in a car, camper, motel, or with another person, there may not be a paper trail to follow.
- Subject may have been abandoned at birth and no correct record of birth may exist. In rural areas children were born at home, not at a hospital. In older days a birth certificate may not have been issued until the child was grown. The date of birth may not be accurate.

CHAPTER II - COURT SYSTEMS

All states as well as the federal government operate court systems. The state court systems are not uniform; that is, the structure of the court system in each state is different. However, there is a certain uniformity in jargon, types of courts, crimes, and records keeping. The records of the courts are most important to the searcher.

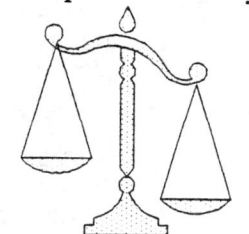

There are essentially two types of courts:

1. Criminal
2. Civil

A court of record maintains a verbatim transcript of the proceedings of a trial along with all other pertinent information about the case. There is usually, but not always, a jury rendering a verdict.

A court of no record does not maintain a verbatim transcript of the proceedings of trial. It does keep all other pertinent information about the case. There is usually no jury to render a verdict. They may also conduct arraignments. This is the point at which most criminal proceedings enter the judicial system.

Everyone is entitled to trial by jury, but, an individual may waive that right. In such a circumstance, law permitting, the case would be decided by the judge hearing the case.

Courts are structured in levels; the lowest court up through the appeals court. Sometimes courts may be called:

- Small Claims Courts
- Circuit Courts
- County Courts
- City Courts
- Superior Courts
- Appellate Courts
- Supreme Courts

- Probate Courts
- Juvenile Courts
- Chancery Courts
- General Sessions Courts
- Civil Courts
- Traffic Courts Etc.

The names of the court usually, but not always, describes the type of court. Some courts with different names may perform the same function. Appeals courts hear appeals on decisions of lower courts. City courts hear cases on small offenses of the city. Juvenile court hears juvenile cases. As a searcher, it is necessary to become familiar with the court system, at least to the extent that a knowledgeable question may be asked of a court official about where to go to find a certain record.

It is not the intent of this book to make the reader an expert on the court system. Rather to show the availability of court records maintained by the court clerks throughout the nation.

COURT RECORDS

The most important thing for the searcher to remember is that all courts keep extremely detailed records. This important function is delegated to the court officer usually called the Clerk of the Court, or Court Clerk, or Clerk and Master. This official is charged with the administrative affairs of the court under the supervision of the judge or judges of that particular court.

The records of these courts are public records. As a searcher, and citizen, you are entitled to the contents of these records. Remember, your tax dollars pay for the entire system.

The great majority of court records are now computerized making access to the information contained within them easily accessible. The court clerks may charge a fee for copies and/or research, in order to defray the cost of their operations. The searcher need only go to the appropriate court clerk and ask for the records desired. In some clerk's offices, computers are available for use by the public in accessing records of the court.

SAMPLE CIRCUIT COURT

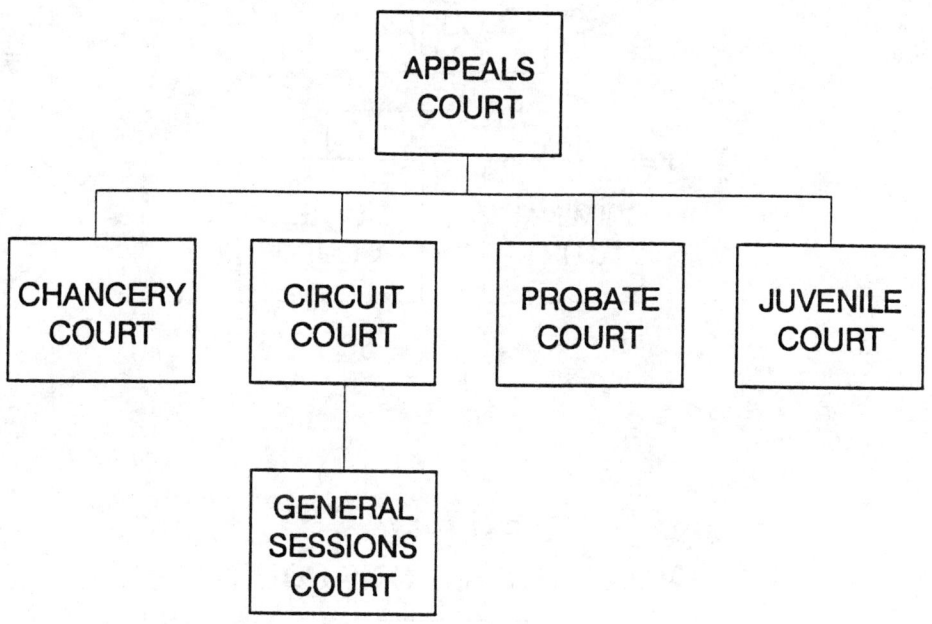

SAMPLE GENERAL SESSIONS COURT

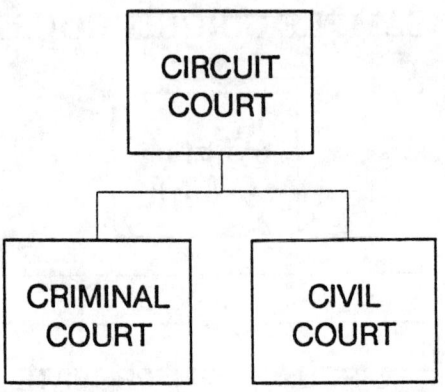

SAMPLE
GENERAL SESSIONS COURT

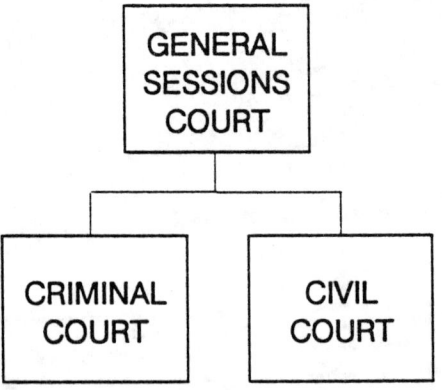

SAMPLE CIVIL COURT CLERK RECORDS

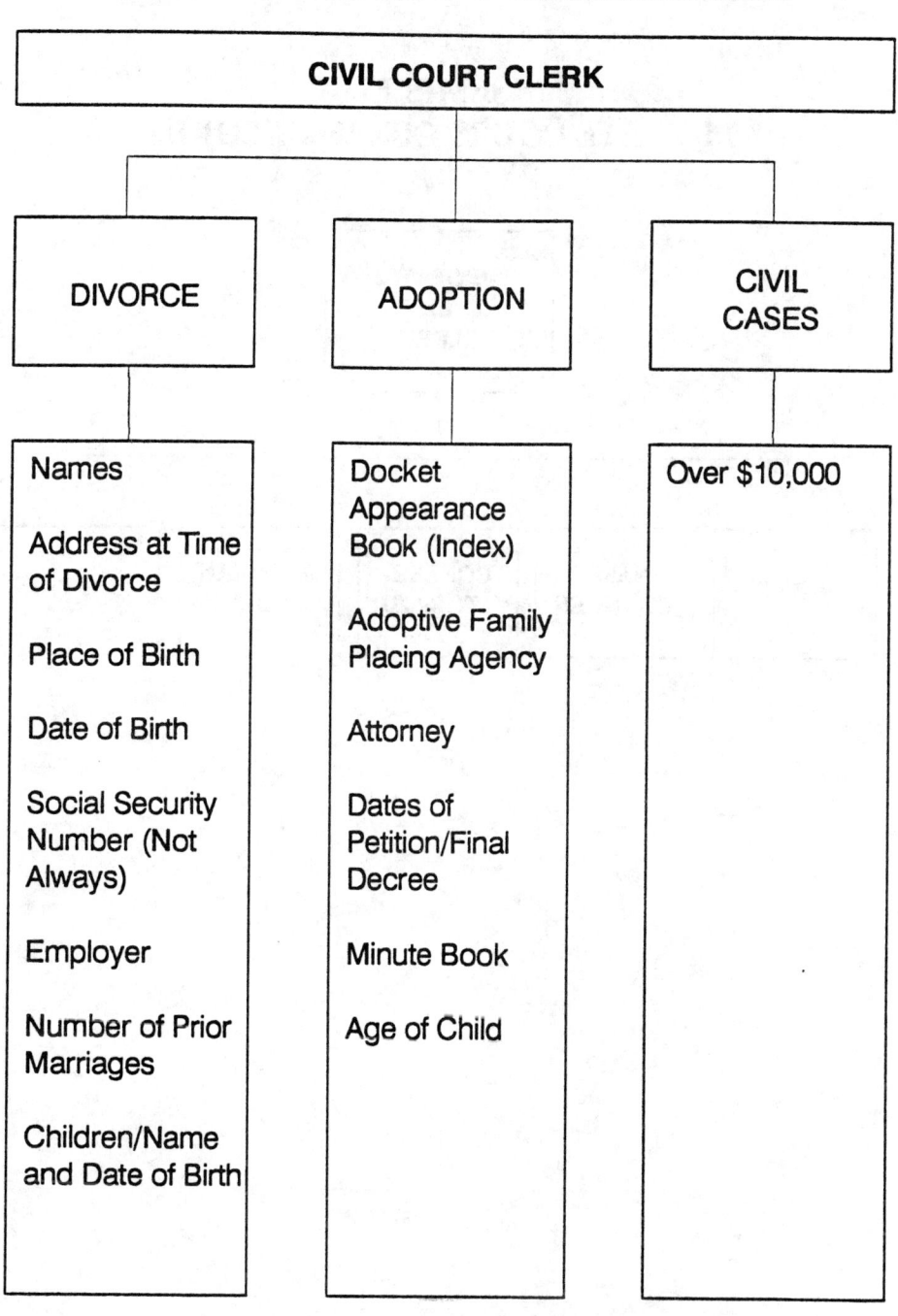

SAMPLE
PROBATE COURT CLERK RECORDS

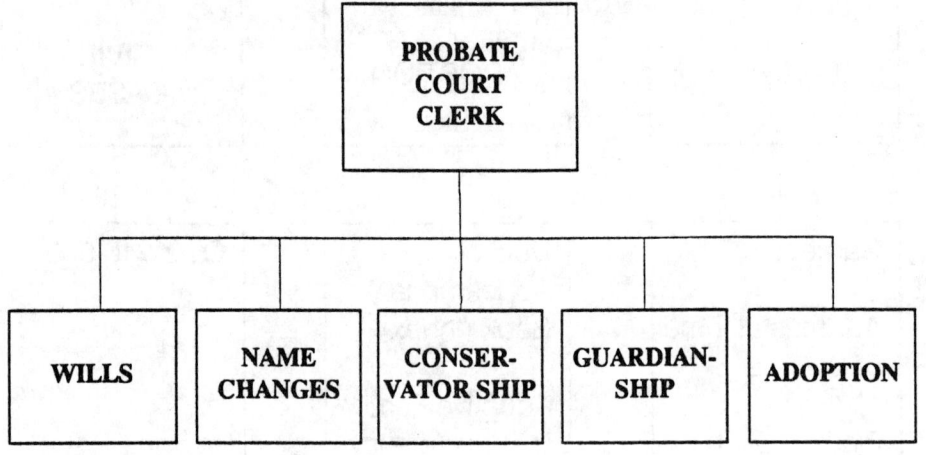

CHAPTER III - RECORDS

In general, all governmental functions throughout the United States, at all levels of government, function in the same manner. That is to say, the functions they perform are precisely the same function as the neighboring government. The various courts, counties, states, townships, cities, and all of their agencies, will have similar, but not necessarily the same, names for their various functions. For example, the City Recorder function in Tennessee is known as the City Clerk in most other states. Another example from Tennessee has the County Clerk registering automobiles, but in some other states this function may be called the Registrar of Vehicles. The searcher should not be confused by such minor differences. Every government must perform the same function as the next. You the searcher need only to ask in order to find out. Since this book is written in Tennessee, titles of the various functionaries as used in Tennessee are used herein. Just as different makes of automobiles may have various functions and may be called by other names, the same basic operation of the vehicle exists.

You will also notice some duplication of functions of records. This is especially true for birth, death, marriage and divorce. This is because entry into the records is generally made in the local jurisdiction where the event occurred. An official certificate should be on file in the locality where the event occurred but it may not be. However, these vital records should be consolidated permanently in a state vital statistics office or in a city, county, or other office.

A publication titled "Where to Write for Vital Records", is published by the National Center for Health Statistics (NCHS). (See Chapter X.) This publication contains the addresses of all locations in the U.S. to write in order to obtain birth, death, marriage, and divorce records. It is available for sale by the:

Superintendent of Documents
U.S. Government Printing Office
Washington, D.C. 20204

The examples listed will provide insight to the reader with respect to what records are used for what purpose, how to search and so on. Remember that local records mean that the records are local to the location where the event happened. In other words a birth in Detroit is a local record in Detroit. A death in Omaha is a local record in Omaha."Local" is not restricted to your location, rather it is the locality of the event.

NOTE: Computer data base information services are available through U.F.O., Inc.

A. DIRECTORIES

1. City Directory

The City Directory is also known as the R.L. Polk Directory. This is one of the most important and most often used references available. It is produced annually by a commercial company and is for sale to the general public. The current, and some previous editions, will be found for that city in the reference section of the public library. The state archive library will have complete sets for the state. Directories for all U.S. cities with populations exceeding 50,000 are available. Your library may have only the directory for your city, but it is possible to call the reference librarian of the city concerned and obtain the desired information.

The City Directory may be accessed through four indices:

» Name
» Phone Number (listed numbers only)
» Address
» Business

If you have either a name, phone number, or address, you need only access the proper index in the directory and it will provide the missing part of your information. For example: if you have an address, access the address index to find the phone number and name for that address. Additional example: if you have a phone number access the number index and find the address, including zip code information for that number. The index for names will provide the missing person's occupation and employer. The directory also has a business index. The business is shown by title and contains information such as corporate officers, proprietors, etc. The business indices lists all businesses by title.

EXAMPLE: Vicki R. had a name and wanted to locate her biological mother. By searching the R.L. Polk directories for the year Vicki was born (1938), she was able to obtain the names of all the families who lived in that city with the same last name as that of her birth mother. She traced each family through the Polk directories for each year until she found the right one. By locating these families she was able to find not only her birth mother but 16 other relatives as well.

The City directory may be purchased through:

» R. L. Polk & Co.
   6400 Monroe Boulevard
   Taylor, MI 48180
   (313) 292-3200

2. Cross-Reference (CRISSCROSS) Directory

The Cross Reference Directory (CRISSCROSS Directory) is another primary reference available to the searcher. It is strictly a directory of street addresses and telephone numbers. This directory is another commercial publication available for use at your local reference library and is also available for purchase. It is similar to the City Directory but does not contain business and employment information. It is published semi-annually. This directory contains two indices: address and telephone number (if not unlisted). An address will give a phone number, or a phone number will give an address. The address will show the number of years a resident has lived at that address. This information is valuable because it will tell the searcher the neighbor who has lived the longest near the missing person. This person can usually provide additional information about the missing person. Just looking the CRISSCROSS directory, find the neighbor, call, and request information. If the telephone number is unlisted, it will not appear. In that case other neighbors may provide the number, or other information, if approached properly.

The Cross Reference Directory may be purchased through:

» City Publishing Company, Inc.
118 South 8th
Independence, KS 67301
(316) 331-2650

3. Directory Assistance

When using directory assistance, the operator will furnish you with no more than three pieces of information for each call. The operator will check the entire area code if requested to do so. When talking to the operator ask her not to cut you off until you are through making requests. Say to the operator, " I have several things I wish you to check on". In this manner, the operator will be stopped from placing your request into the automatic assistance machine forcing you to call back. The more information the operator has the better the results will be. For example: you may ask for Smith with an "i" or a "y", and Jones on Elm Street in one call. This service is available through the normal assistance operator or the "800" operator.

To access directory assistance dial:

1 (area code) 555-1212
1 (800) 555-1212

EXAMPLE: A private investigator approached U.F.O. requesting assistance in a background investigation concerning Greg S. He knew only Greg's name and Social Security Number (SSN). He needed to complete a criminal history check on Greg. The investigator knew that Greg currently lived in Tennessee and that Greg had formerly resided in Indiana. The investigator needed to know where Greg had lived in Indiana. U.F.O. ran the SSN on the computer data base and found Greg's last three addresses in Tennessee. However, the computer did not disclose any address for Greg in Indiana. Again using Greg's SSN another search was initiated using, current address and Zip, and full name. Within seconds the information data base furnished an address in Plymouth, Indiana. Plymouth was located by map near South Bend. The phone book showed 219 as the area code for South Bend. Dialing (1) (219) 555-1212 the directory assistance operator for South Bend was contacted. The operator asked "What city?" I replied "Plymouth. Could you please tell me the county seat for Plymouth? I need the courthouse, the criminal court clerk's number." Within seconds the operator furnished the number. The entire operation lasted only minutes. The private investigator could now run the criminal check on Greg with one phone call. Directory assistance saved the private investigator, and his client, both time and money.

TECHNIQUE: When requesting a name from directory assistance but the city is unknown, ask the operator to check the entire area code. It is not necessary to have an address for the operator to look up a number.

TECHNIQUE: When speaking to directory assistance operators, ask for the name on "Broad" street. The operator will often respond, "We have the name on Main street but not on "Broad" street". This way you get the correct street name which was not known previously.

B. LOCAL

1. County Clerk Records

Every county has a County Clerk. This official is charged with all manner of record keeping and recording. Recordings of liens, documents such as wills or records of military service are maintained by the clerk. Do not confuse the County Clerk  with a Court Clerk. This person is usually elected to perform certain statutory functions and is not to be confused with the court system. Court records are not maintained by the County Clerk. In some states the County Clerk may collect taxes. In others there may be an official known as the Trustee, or some other name, who collects taxes.

This official issues:

>   Marriage Licenses
>   Business License/Taxes
>   Vehicle Licenses and Titles

This official records:

>   Wills
>   Committals
>   Estates
>   Business License
>   Liens
>   Document Recording
>   Etc., any manner of document anyone may wish to record and preserve.

In many cases an application accompanied by a fee is required in order to obtain document copies. In most states these are all public records and each local authority will have a procedure for accessing these records.

EXAMPLE: I needed to locate Melissa M. who formerly was a partner in a beauty shop that had gone out of business. By obtaining the beauty shop's business license I was able to locate a previous partner who told me where Melissa had moved.

2. **Voter Registration**

The voter registration records are important to the searcher because they may contain the SSN of each registered voter. The voter registration records are maintained in each county by a person usually known as the Voter Registrar, Commissioner of Elections, or some other similar title. Care must be taken when using these records. In order to register to vote, most states require only something with a name and address as identification. An envelope with a name and address is sometimes sufficient. Such documentation could also be any receipt showing name and address. All of the information could be false. Very rarely is the information verified. There will be a place to enter a SSN, but if not checked, it's validity may be uncertain. A fee may or may not be required to obtain this information. The information on the application may vary, but as a very minimum, there will usually be:

    Name
    Address
    Telephone number
    Employer
    Place of birth
    Date of birth
    Social Security Number

3. **Marriage License**

Official certificates of birth, death, marriage, and divorce will be on file where the event occurred. Marriage licenses are usually issued by the city or county clerk. The federal government does not maintain statistics or files on these records. They will be filed permanently in a city, county, or state vital statistics bureau. In order to obtain a copy of the certificates, go to the state office or area where the event occurred and make application. There may be a fee. The records will show:

>Name(s)
>Date License Issued
>Addresses

4. **Occupational License**

The practice of licensing tradesmen and professionals is widespread. Most professionals such as doctors, lawyers, dentists, etc, are licensed by the state. However, tradesmen such as plumbers, carpenters, locksmiths, etc, are licensed at the city or county level; mostly depending upon the population of the city or county. These records can generally be accessed by:

>Occupation
>Name of Business
>Name
>Address

5. **Tax Assessor**

Every county has a tax assessor. Usually the tax assessor collects both county and state taxes forwarding the state share of the revenue to the state. If the missing person owns property in that county, it will be reflected in the records of the Tax Assessor. At the assessor's office, computer data bases, microfiche, and/or record books are available showing a history of ownership. These records show mailing addresses and other information which may be used to track down missing persons. Information contained in the Tax Assessor records will include:

- Property Owned
- Date Acquired
- Value
- Previous Owners
- Address the Tax Bill Goes To
- Partners
- Address of the Owners
- Real Estate Agent
- Mortgage Holder

EXAMPLE: I needed to locate Charles E. He owned rental property but lived in another state. I went to the office of the Tax Assessor and looked up the property owned by Charles E. The records disclosed the address where the tax bill was sent. Charles E. was found at that address.

6. **Registrar of Deeds**

Property records are a county function. In some counties the County Clerk or Tax Assessor may perform this function. These records will show:

- Address of Owners

Property Owned
Mortgage or Finance Company
Attorneys Participating
Real Estate Company
Insurance Company

EXAMPLE: I was searching for Barbara A. I knew she formerly worked in Gallatin, Tennessee. I went to the court house and looked up property in his name. The property had been sold by a real estate company and was now owned by another family. The name of the real estate company was listed in the records. I located the real estate agent who conducted the sale and he gave me Barbara's current address.

7. **Vehicle Registration Records**

    The County Clerk, or equivalent, will have records for any type of vehicle registered in that county. This includes boats, trailers, and motorcycles, etc. At the county level the records may be accessed by name or license number. The records may reveal co-owners or spouses. A title  search will show who the vehicle was purchased from, how it was financed, any liens, previous licenses, etc. Each state maintains a consolidated record of vehicle registration records from all of its counties.

    EXAMPLE: Microfiche of all people who own vehicles by both alpha and numerical may be bought in some states. Whenever I need to locate someone, I first check the alpha microfiche to see if they own a vehicle and if so, I have the address, license tag, make, and model of the vehicle.

8. **School Records**

Nearly all schools and colleges issue yearbooks. Usually a copy of all yearbooks issued previously are maintained in the school library. Colleges and universities will have alumni associations which maintain separate records. The yearbooks may include information pertaining to the interests of the missing person which may provide an additional place to search. The names of students and parents of students who attended government (city, county, and state) schools are a matter of public record although other information contained within these records may not be. The reference section of the public library will contain a copy of Patterson's American Education. This book lists all universities, colleges, junior colleges, high schools, grammar schools, and private schools in the United States. Always check the alumni association. The Board of Education may, or may not, help.

9. **Local Library Reference Librarian**

There is usually at least one person in the reference section of your local library who is extremely knowledgeable about any type of reference material. Much material is available on microfiche, microfilm, or computer. It is an excellent investment to visit the reference section of your local library.

TECHNIQUE: The reference section of Main Public Libraries are a "gold mine" of information. Old newspapers are on microfilm. By looking up obituaries, survivors may be located. By looking up a subject title, all articles pertaining to that subject may be located. Telephone directories for all states are available. The reference librarian is usually very helpful and once you explain exactly what you need, the librarian will show you or tell you what you need to do. I have contacted reference librarians in many states by telephone and requested they search for information at their convenience and call me back collect. I have only been refused once.

10. Churches and Clubs

As indicated before, missing persons seldom change their habits. A catholic stays with the catholic church and a Presbyterian stays with that church. A rotarian will remain a rotarian. These groups and organizations maintain membership rosters and directories which are used for mailing purposes.
Many groups now maintain these rosters on computers. These rosters will generally show:

>   Name
>   Address
>   Telephone Number
>   Occupation
>   Work Address

11. Newspapers

A valuable source of information, newspapers maintain files and photo-graphs by subject, name, and date. Most have long histories. Most are on microfilm or microfiche. They often maintain librarians, who like the public library reference librarian, can provide invaluable assistance. It is truly amazing the amount of information and history contained in newspaper files.

12. Credit Reports

I have included credit reports at the local level because credit bureaus and other credit reporting agencies are available to the searcher everywhere. These reports are available on anyone, anywhere, who has ever used credit for anything. Access is limited to lawful purposes and may require that the individual concerned sign a release of information form. The searcher must be familiar with the Fair Credit Reporting Act; a Federal Law. (See Chapter IX).

EXAMPLE: An attorney needed to locate Don R. after obtaining a judgement against him. Don had moved not leaving a forwarding address. Under the "Fair Credit Reporting Act", a credit report may be requested by a qualified person or agency under certain conditions without a release from the individual concerned. One of these conditions is for collection purposes. By running a credit report on Don through my computer database, I found a car dealer's name in Atlanta, GA who had also run a credit report on him. By contacting the car dealership, I was able to talk with the salesman who had just sold Don a new car. The salesman told me where Don lived and worked. I contacted the employer to verify employment. The employer verified the new address given to me by the car salesman.

C. COURT RECORDS

1. Traffic

A traffic ticket will usually contain:

- Driver's license number
- Social Security number
- Employer
- Type of vehicle
- Name of issuing officer
- Driver's license information

Records on traffic and parking violations are maintained by cities and counties. They are maintained at the place where traffic fines are paid. These records may be accessed by name only in some states. Some states may require date of birth (DOB) or DL number. The parking ticket will not contain a name, but you can determine who paid the ticket. Whoever paid the ticket will probably lead you to the missing person. There may or may not be a fee for this service. Bear in mind that there may be more than one ticket or fine, so ask for all information concerning the missing person. This will include the number of violations and disposition such as traffic school, fine, bonds-man, etc.

2. **Circuit Court**

Circuit court records include:

   Divorce
   Adoption
   Marriage
   Civil Suits (sometimes)
   Probate (sometimes)

Circuit court is located at the county seat of each respective county and is easily contacted by telephone. Circuit courts do not normally handle traffic or other similar offenses. Nearly all of these records are now computerized. A name search will show a docket number and/or case file number. The searcher need only make a request to the court clerk for that case and/or file number to see the entire file. This is not privileged information. These are all records of court proceedings in public session. As such, anyone appearing in court is recorded in these records. These records disclose the attorneys concerned, witnesses, addresses, charges, disposition, dates and gives SSN, dates of birth, employer, property owned, all manner of information. The information is nearly limitless. In short, everything about and pertaining to each case is contained in the record for that case. A fee is normally charged for each copy. Requests in writing, accompanied by the fee, may be made by mail. These mail requests will usually be honored. Verification may be made by phone.

EXAMPLE: Terri T. wished to locate her father. Her parents were divorced when Terri T. was one year old. Her mother is now deceased. Terri knew the name of her father shown on her birth certificate. She contacted U.F.O. with only the name. Terri assumed the divorce was granted in Nashville, TN (Davidson County) because that was where her mother and she lived at the time of the divorce. Divorces are usually granted by the circuit court of the county of residence. There are exceptions but this is the norm. U.F.O. used the phone to contact the circuit court clerk for Davidson County requesting a search for both the mother and father of Terri to verify if the divorce had in fact been granted in Davidson County. It was verified and the case file number was furnished immediately. U.F.O. went personally to the office of the circuit court clerk, asked for the case number, and within a matter of minutes was viewing the file. The date, place of birth, and SSN of the father, also his employer and address at time of the divorce, previous marriages and dates, names of children and their dates of birth, were disclosed. Importantly, the record also showed where and when this marriage took place. Terri was able to locate her father using the information contained in the divorce case records.

Divorce Records

These records normally are found at the circuit court of the county of residence though in some states it is not mandatory. Requirements vary by state.

EXAMPLE: John B. was only two years old when his parents divorced. His mother hated his father and did not want child support because she did not want the father to ever see his son again; not even visitation rights. The father was never allowed to see his son again. The mother remarried and changed John's last name. John grew up without knowing his father, John, Sr., but always wanted to. John's mother would never discuss the father, it was a taboo subject. At the age of twenty John decided to search for his father, but had very little information to work with. He found a picture of his father in the attic. The picture was taken in Germany in 1945 in the Army. On the back of the picture was a name; John Samuel B. With only this information John spent 20 years searching for his father without success. John was 40 years old when he asked me to help locate his father. The first thing I did was go to the court house to the clerk of circuit court. There I accessed the records to find the parents divorce decree. The records showed that divorce papers for John Samuel B. were mailed to an address in a small town in Florida. The B. family house was still in Florida, but the family had been gone for several years. By talking with the neighbors, I learned that the mother of John Samuel B., Sr. previously owned the property at that address, but had died five years ago. Nothing else about the family was known. Knowing that many people leave wills and that these wills are probated in county courts, I went to the county seat. I went to probate court and looked up all wills in the name of "B" for the past five years. I was looking for the survivors of a female named "B". I quickly located the probate record of a woman from the same small town whose survivors listed a son named John Samuel B. at the address. It also listed a daughter named Nancy M. at an address in a nearby town. I looked up an M. family in the small town phone directory and drove there. The woman who answered the door was Nancy, the sister of John's father and called John's father the next day. John and his father were reunited immediately. The 1950 paper trail left in a Nashville divorce court took me to a 1970 paper trail in a Florida probate court which led me to the missing person who was in South Carolina.

Total time of investigation: 9 days.

3. **Criminal Court**

Criminal court records include:

> Warrants
> Criminal Histories

The office of the criminal court clerk can easily be contacted by telephone. Once a criminal has been arrested he will appear in criminal court. Everyone who appears in court, even though the case may be dismissed, will appear on a record called the Docket Appearance Book, or something very similar. The legal system for every state requires very specific records using very specific procedures be maintained by each court. It is the job of the court clerk to properly maintain these records under the supervision of the judges of the courts they serve. These records and procedures are established by various state statutes. Therefore the information contained within these records will be most specific as to form and content. These records are now mostly computerized making access quick and easy. A searcher needs a name and date of birth (and/or docket number) for the clerk to find the proper record. A small fee is usually required. Once the record is identified, the clerk will run a print out from the computer on the individual concerned. For every arrest a warrant is required. Once the person has appeared in court, the warrant number will be included in the court records. The warrant contains:

> Name of person arrested
> Date of birth
> Address
> Physical description
> Offense
> Arresting officer
> Prosecutor
> Bondsman

The information contained on the police reports is normally not available to the public, but once the person has been arrested he/she must appear in court. At that time the information from the police records will become a part of the criminal court record and will contain much of the information that the police records contain. All courts are public bodies. No one may be tried and sentenced in secret. One need only to take advantage of this public record. The searcher may speak to any of the persons named on the warrant such as the arresting officer or prosecutor. These persons, at their discretion, can answer any questions the searcher may care to ask.

EXAMPLE: David M. had jumped a $25,000 bail bond. The Nashville bondsman would either have to produce David in court or pay the $25,000 bond. David told the bondsman he lived in Columbus, Ohio. Bondsmen require collateral for their bonds; preferably real property. His parents had collateralized his bond as they owned property and resided in Columbus, Ohio. With the information furnished by the bondsman, U.F.O. travelled to Columbus, Ohio to the office of the criminal court clerk at the county courthouse. Their records were computer-ized. The court clerk staff assisted in operating the computer. Their records showed two outstanding warrants on David. The warrants revealed a female victim who had been kidnapped by David. The address of the victim, was listed on the warrant. U.F.O. then went to the listed address finding still there. She confided that David was living in Nelsonville, Ohio with another woman. U.F.O. then went to the police station at Nelsonville, and showed a photo of David which had been furnished by the bondsman. The policemen knew the individual and exactly where he lived. U.F.O. advised the policemen that David was wanted in Ohio as well as Tennessee. He was arrested by the Nelsonville police department. Jurisdiction was claimed by Ohio authorities and the bondsman did not lose his $25,000 bond. David M. had three identities, three names, three SSNs, and three dates of birth. He was caught by using his paper trail.

4. **Chancery Court (where applicable)**

These records will include:

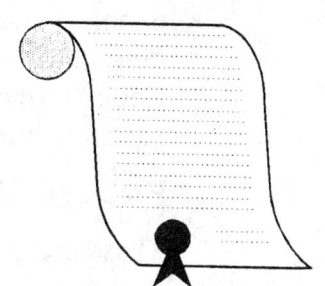

> Lawsuits
> Judgments
> Liens
> Divorce
> Contracts
> Name Changes
> Adoptions
> Debts
> Appeals (from lower courts or arbitrators)

In many cases an application accompanied by a fee is required in order to obtain document copies. However, these are all public records and each local authority will have a procedure for accessing these records.

EXAMPLE: I am searching for a daughter who was adopted in 1951. There is an index book of all adoptive families who appeared in court to adopt children. This book is also called a Docket Appearance Book (or Docket) and may be found in various court clerk's offices depending on the year and the court of jurisdiction. The docket appearance book gives information regarding the filing of a petition as well as a final decree and other records. Several steps must be taken before an adoption is final. (See Chapter XII). Each step is recorded in a record called a Minute Book. In this case, Tennessee law does not make the Minute Book confidential and does not require a consent form or court order for access. Also, in this particular case, the minute book concerned was the minute book for adoptions only. States have their own adoption laws so the Minute Book (or Docket Book) may or may not require consent or court order. By understanding the adoption process, the laws pertaining to adoption for the year of the search and the court system, in many states a paper trail is available on public records. By process of elimination it is possible to locate the adoptee. This is a very time-consuming and frustrating search, but it is not impossible. Be prepared to spend a lot of time running down the many leads which are found in the Docket Book. I advise anyone searching for an adoptee or birth parent to attend my seminars. See Chapter XII.

5. **Probate Court**

    These records will include:

    > Wills
    > Adoptions
    > Older Adoptions
    > Mental committals
    > Conservatorship
    > Guardianship
    > Name Changes

    This court hears and decides cases of a "personal" nature, rather than civil or criminal problems. Here is where "human tragedy" may be resolved. The death of a relative or friend may leave a will. A beloved aunt may have alzheimer disease requiring a guardian or committal.

    In many cases an application accompanied by a fee is required in order to obtain document copies. Here too, each local authority will have a procedure and, perhaps, a fee for accessing these records.

    Probate records are very complete due to requirements of the court. Probate records are completed actions that the court took with regard to persons who are dead or who are unable to handle their personal affairs.

D. STATE RECORDS

Official certificates of birth, death, marriage, and divorce will be on file where the event occurred. The federal government does not maintain statistics or files on these records. They will be filed permanently in a city, county, or state vital statistics bureau. In order to obtain a copy of the certificates, go to the state office or  area where the event occurred and make application. Some states will search by name, but will release the information only to next of kin or relative. There maybe a fee.

1. Birth Certificate

The records will show:

> Mother's Name
> Father's Name
> Place of Birth (including the hospital)
> Name of the Baby
> Finger or Footprints (sometimes)
> Attending Physician

2. Death Certificate

There is no cross reference available to cross reference births with deaths. (That is how people can get by with using more than one SSN or change identities.) The searcher must usually have full name and date of death. Death record searches of all deaths after 1962 are available, nationwide by individual name, or family name, through the U.F.O. data base. The Social Security Administration maintains a death record file. The searcher need not have full name and date of death. An official death certificate should show:

> Name
> Address at time of death
> Place of death
> Cause of death

Date of death
Attending physician or coroner

Death record computer searches made through U.F.O. should include:

Name
Place of death
Date of birth
Date of death
Place of birth
Social Security Number

3. **Vehicle Registration**

These records will show any liens outstanding on the vehicle, former owners, any financing, former tags, and the current owner and address. Information included will be:

Owner
Address
Title/History
Liens or co-owners
Vehicle Identification Number (VIN)

STATE MOTOR VEHICLE REGISTRATION OFFICES

ALABAMA
Title Section
2721 Gunter Park Drive
P.O. Box 1331
Montgomery, AL 36102
(205) 271-3250

ALASKA
Department of Public Safety
Motor Vehicle Division
Attn: Research
5700 East Tudor Road
Anchorage, AK 99507

ARKANSAS
Office of Motor Vehicles
P.O. Box 1272
Little Rock, AR 72203

ARIZONA
Motor Vehicle Division
Title Records
1801 West Jefferson Avenue
Phoenix, AZ 85007

CALIFORNIA
State of California
Department of Motor Vehicles
P.O. Box 944247
Sacramento, CA 94244-2470
(916) 732-7243

COLORADO
Title Section
140 West 6th Avenue
Denver, CO 80204
(303) 620-4108

CONNECTICUT
Division of Motor Vehicles
60 State Street
Wethersfield, CT 06109
(203) 566-4410

DELAWARE
Division of Motor Vehicles
Attn: Correspondence Pool
P.O. Box 698
Dover, DE 19903
(302) 736-3147

DISTRICT OF COLUMBIA
Bureau of Motor Vehicle Services
301 C Street NW
Washington, DC 20001
(202) 727-6680

FLORIDA
Division of Motor Vehicles
Neil Kirman Building
Tallahassee, FL 32301
(904) 488-4127

GEORGIA
Motor Vehicle Division
126 Trinity-Washington Building
Atlanta, GA 30334
(404) 656-4100

IDAHO
Idaho Transportation Department
Vehicle Research
Box 34
Boise, ID 83707
(208) 334-8663

INDIANA
Bureau of Motor Vehicles
401 State Office Building
100 North Senate Avenue
Indianapolis, IN 46204
(317) 232-2798

KANSAS
Department of Revenue
Division of Vehicles
State Office Building
Topeka, KS 66626
(913) 296-3621

LOUISIANA
Office of Motor Vehicles
Department of Public Safety
P.O. Box 64886
Baton Rouge, LA 70896
(504) 925-6146

HAWAII
Division of Motor Vehicle
Licensing
1455 South Beretania Street
Honolulu, HI 96814
(808) 955-8221

ILLINOIS
Secretary of State
Vehicle Records Inquiry Sec.
4th Floor, Centennial Bldg.
Springfield, IL 62756
(217) 782-6992

IOWA
Dept. of Transportation
Office of Vehicle Registration
Lucas State Office Building
Des Moines, IA 50319
(515) 281-7710

KENTUCKY
Department of Vehicle
Registration
Motor Vehicle Licensing
New State Office Building
Frankfort, KY 40622
(502) 564-7570

MAINE
Department of State
Motor Vehicle Division
State House Station 29
Augusta, ME 04333
(207) 289-3071

MARYLAND
Motor Vehicle Administration
6601 Ritchie Highway, NE
Glen Burnie, MD 21062
(301) 768-7000

MICHIGAN
Department of State
Bureau of Driver & Vehicle Services
7064 Crowner Drive
Lansing, MI 48918
(517) 322-1166

MISSISSIPPI
Department of Motor Vehicles
P.O. Box 1140
Jackson, MS 39205
(601) 359-1248

MONTANA
Registrar's Bureau
925 Main Street
Deer Lodge, MT 58722
(406) 846-1423

NEVADA
Department of Motor Vehicles
Registration Division
Carson City, NV 89711
(702) 855-5370

NEW JERSEY
Bureau of Office Services
Certified Information Unit
25 South Montgomery Street
Trenton, NJ 08666
(609) 292-4102

MASSACHUSETTS
Registrar of Motor Vehicles
100 Nashua Street
Boston, MA 02114
(617) 727-3700

MINNESOTA
Department of Public Safety
Driver and Vehicle Services
Transportation Building
St. Paul, MN 55155
(612) 296-6911

MISSOURI
Motor Vehicle Bureau
P.O. Box 100
Jefferson City, MO 65701
(314) 751-4509

NEBRASKA
Dept. of Motor Vehicles
P.O. Box 94789
Lincoln, NE 68509
(402) 471-2281

NEW HAMPSHIRE
Department of Safety
Division of Motor Vehicles
J. H. Hayes Building
Concord, NH 03305
(603) 271-2251

NEW MEXICO
Motor Vehicles Division
P.O. Box 1028
Santa Fe, NM 87504
(505) 827-2173

NEW YORK
Department of Motor Vehicles
Empire Plaza
Albany, NY 12228
(518) 474-2121

NORTH DAKOTA
Motor Vehicles Department
Capitol Grounds
Bismark, ND 58505
(701) 224-2725

OKLAHOMA
Motor Vehicle Division
2501 Lincoln Blvd.
Oklahoma City, OK 73194
(405) 521-3221

PENNSYLVANIA
Bureau of Motor Vehicles
Transportation & Safety Building
Harrisburg, PA 17122
(717) 787-3130

SOUTH CAROLINA
Motor Vehicle Division
Dept. of Highway & Public
Transportation
Columbia, SC 29216

TENNESSEE
Motor Vehicle Division
500 Deaderick Street
Nashville, TN 37242
(615) 741-3101

NORTH CAROLINA
Vehicle Registration
Division of Motor Vehicles
1100 New Bern Avenue
Raleigh, NC 27697
(919) 733-3025

OHIO
Dept. of Highway Safety
Bureau of Motor Vehicles
P.O. Box 16520
Columbus, OH 43216
(614) 752-7500

OREGON
Motor Vehicle Division
1905 Lana Avenue, NE
Salem, OR 97314
(503) 371-2200

RHODE ISLAND
Registrar of Motor Vehicles
State Office Building
Providence, RI 02903
(401) 277-2970

SOUTH DAKOTA
Department of Revenue
118 West Capitol
Pierre, SD 57501
(605) 773-3541

TEXAS
Department of Highway &
Public Transportation
40th & Jackson Avenue
Austin, TX 78779
(512) 465-7611

UTAH
State Tax Commission
Motor Vehicle Division
State Fair Grounds
1905 Motor Avenue
Salt Lake City, UT 84416
(801) 538-8300

VIRGINIA
Department of Motor Vehicles
P.O. Box 27412
Richmond, VA 23269
(804) 367-0523

WEST VIRGINIA
Department of Motor Vehicles
State Capitol Complex, Building 3
Charleston, WV 2531
(304) 348-3900

WYOMING
Department of Revenue
Motor Vehicle Division
122 West 25th Street
Cheyenne, WY 82202

VERMONT
Department of Motor Vehicles
120 State Street
Montpelier, VT 05603
(802) 828-2000

WASHINGTON
Department of Licensing
P.O. Box 9909
Olympia, WA 98504
(206) 753-6946

WISCONSIN
Registration Files
WI Dept. of Transportation
P.O. Box 7909
Madison, WI 53707
(608) 266-1466

4. Driver's License/Driving History

Both the driver's license and the driving history are available. The information generally available through this paper trail is:

Driver's License

> Full Name
> Address
> Driver's License Number
> (In some states the driver's license number is the social security number)
> Physical Description
> Date of Birth (DOB)

Driving History

> Accidents
> Traffic and Parking Tickets
> Other Vehicles
> Investigating Officer

Using the paper trail, a follow-up paper trail may be developed to lead to other vehicles the missing person may have driven. Traffic tickets and accident reports contain much information. An insurance company or hospital record may be indicated which may, in turn, provide additional information for the paper trail. Court dates, arresting officer, warrants, employers - the information trail is limitless.

TECHNIQUE: By obtaining a copy of a driving history, it is possible to track accident reports, traffic tickets, and vehicles the person may drive. In searching for a missing person, one of the first things I do is check for a driver's license. Most states require both a name and date of birth (D.O.B.). Some states require a written request for the information; however, most states have information available through a computer database search.

STATE DRIVERS LICENSE OFFICES

Most states will require a full name and date of birth when requesting drivers license information. A written request should be accompanied by a check for the amount involved. To determine the cost a phone call to the appropriate office may be necessary. As long as you are checking on a driver's license, you might as well ask for the driving history. A few states may require you register before allowing you this information.

ALABAMA
Drivers License Division
Certificate Section
P.O. Box 1471
Montgomery, AL 36192

ALASKA
Department of Public Safety
Drivers License Safety
Pouch N
Juneau, AK 99801

ARIZONA
Motor Vehicle Division
1801 West Jefferson Street
Phoenix, AZ 85007

ARKANSAS
Office of Drivers Services
Traffic Violation Report Unit
P.O. Box 1272
Little Rock, AR 72203

CALIFORNIA
Department of Motor Vehicles
P.O. Box 944247
Sacramento, CA 94244-2470

COLORADO
Traffic Records Section
140 West 6th Avenue
Room 103
Denver, CO 80204

CONNECTICUT
Department of Motor Vehicles
Record Section
60 State Street
Wethersfield, CT 06209

DELAWARE
Department of Public
SafetyMotor Vehicles
DivisionP.O. Box 698Dover,
DE 19901

DISTRICT OF COLUMBIA
Bureau of Motor Vehicle Services
301 C StreetNW
Washington, DC 20001

FLORIDA
Dept. of Highway Safety
Drivers License Division
Kirkhaam Building
Tallahassee, FL 32301

HAWAII
Violations Bureau
824 Bethel
Honolulu, HI 96813

IOWA
Department of Transportation
Office of Driver's Services
Lucas State Office Building
Des Moines, IA 50319

KENTUCKY
Division of Driver Licenses
State Office Building
Frankfort, KY 40622

MAINE
Department of State
Motor Vehicle Division
State House Station 29
Augusta, ME 04333

MASSACHUSETTS
Registry of Motor Vehicles
100 Nashua Street
Boston, MA 02114

MINNESOTA
Department of Public Safety
Drivers License Division
Room 108 State Highway Building
St. Paul, MN 55155

ILLINOIS
Secretary of State
Drivers Service Section
2701 South Dirksen Parkway
Springfield, IL 62723

KANSAS
Division of Vehicles
Driver Control Bureau
State Office Building
Topeka, KS 66626

LOUISIANA
Department of Public Safety
Office of Motor Vehicles
Box 64886
Baton Rouge, LA 70896

MARYLAND
Motor Vehicle
Administration
6601 Ritchie Highway NE
Glen Burnie, MD 21062

MICHIGAN
Department of State
Driver & Vehicle Services
7064 Crowner Drive
Lansing, MI 49818

MISSISSIPPI
Mississippi Highway Safety
Patrol
Drivers License Division
P.O. Box 958
Jackson, MS 39205

MISSOURI
Bureau of Driver Licenses
P.O. Box 200
Department of Revenue
Jefferson City, MO 65101

NEBRASKA
Department of Motor Vehicles
Driver Records Section
P.O. Box 94789
Lincoln, NE 68509

NEW HAMPSHIRE
Division of Motor Vehicles
Drivers License Division
J. H. Hayes Building
Concord, NH 03305

NEW MEXICO
Motor Vehicle Division
Driver Services Bureau
P.O. Box 1028
Santa Fe, NM 87504

NORTH CAROLINA
Traffic Records Section
Division of Motor Vehicles
1100 New Bern Avenue
Raleigh, NC 27697

OHIO
Bureau of Motor Vehicles
P.O. Box 16520
Columbus, OH 43216

MONTANA
Montana Highway Patrol
303 North Roberts
Helena, MT 59620

NEVADA
Department of Motor Vehicles
Drivers License Division
Carson City, NV 89711

NEW JERSEY
Department of Law and Public Safety
Drivers License Division
P.O. Box 7068 West
Trenton, NJ 08628

NEW YORK
Department of Motor Vehicles
Empire State Plaza
Albany, NY 12228

NORTH DAKOTA
Drivers License Department
Capitol Grounds
Bismark, ND 58505

OKLAHOMA
Driver Records Service
Department of Public Safety
P.O. Box 11415
Oklahoma City, OK 73136

OREGON
Motor Vehicle Division1
905 Lona Avenue, NE
Salem, OR 97314

RHODE ISLAND
Registry of Motor Vehicles
Room 101 G
State Office Building
Providence, RI 02903

SOUTH DAKOTA
Department of Commerce and
Regulation
118 West Capitol
Pierre, SD 57501

TEXAS
Driver Records Division
40th & Jackson Avenue
Austin, TX 78779

VERMONT
Department of Motor Vehicles
120 State Street
Montpelier, VT 05602

WASHINGTON
Department of Licensing
P.O. Box 9909
Olympia, WA 98504

PENNSYLVANIA
Dept. of Transportation
Bureau of Drivers Licensing
Transportation & Safety Bldg
Harrisburg, PA 17120

SOUTH CAROLINA
Department of Highways and
Public Transportation
Drivers Records Clerk,
P.O. Box 1498
Columbia, SC 29216

TENNESSEE
Department of Safety
Andrew Jackson Building
5th & Deaderick Street
Nashville, TN 37219

UTAH
Drivers License Division
314 State Office Building
Salt Lake City, UT 84114

VIRGINIA
Dept. of Motor Vehicles
Driver Licensing & Info.
P.O. Box 27412
Richmond, VA 23269

WEST VIRGINIA
Department of Motor
Vehicles8
00 Washington Street
Charleston, WV 25305

WISCONSIN
Department of Transportation
P.O. Box 7918
Madison, WI 53707

WYOMING
Department of Revenue
122 West 25th Street
Cheyenne, WY 82002

5. **Corporations**

   The Secretary of State maintains records of all businesses, profit and non-profit, incorporated under the laws of the state. The records maintained by the Secretary of State include:

   > Officers
   > Annual Reports
   > Incorporating Parties
   > Uniform Commercial Code Filings: Commercial Credit

   In some states there may be a fee for records from this office. The Office of the Secretary of State for Tennessee charges $20.00 for copies of annual reports.

6. **Occupational/Professional License**

   Normally the state will license only professionals. Tradesmen will be licensed at the city or county. However, certain occupations such as Private Investigator, Security Guard, General Contractor, etc, are now being licensed and regulated by the states. The information contained in these records is very complete even to the extent that fingerprints may be on file. These licenses may be found at either the local or state level.

7. **State Police**

   State Police information about ongoing investigations, confidential sources, etc., is not public. However, investigating or arresting officers will sometimes assist the searcher if it does not violate departmental policy. A good deal of tact and circumspect is called for when interviewing police officers. Cooperation from law-enforcement requires the searcher be totally honest and forthright regarding the purpose of the search.

8. Parole and Probation Records

State crimes are tried in courts located in county seats. Some state offenders are housed in county jails while serving sentences for state crimes. All offenders, when placed on probation or paroled, are assigned to the parole officer in the county where the offender will be paroled. The parole officer is an employee of the State Department of Corrections and reports to a superior at the state. However, the parole officer will maintain records of the information on the parolee and should know where the parolee is at all times.

9. State Archives Library

The state archives library contains more information that anyone could ever use. Generally speaking, it contains the history of the state and is not restricted to content.

EXAMPLE: Lisa L. wanted to locate information for genealogy purposes. She had her great-grandfather's name and where he died. By searching the Census Records on microfilm Lisa was able to find other members of the family and complete her search.

10. Workers Compensation Claims

Nearly every state regulates workers compensation insurance. Anyone who ever filed a workers compensation claim should be on file. The information contained on this file will give the nature of injury, employer, doctor, etc. When a claim is made for workers compensation, it is made to the insurance company and winds up in state records. Copies of the claim may be found at the office of the employer, the doctor's office, the insurance agency, and with the claimant. In order to obtain this information, it is necessary to have an authorization from the claimant.

WHERE TO WRITE FOR WORKERS COMPENSATION RECORDS

ALABAMA
Worker's Compensation Division
Industrial Relation Building
Montgomery, AL 36130

ALASKA
Worker's Compensation Div.
P.O. Box 25512
Juneau, AK 99802

ARIZONA
State Compensation Fund
3031 North Second Street
Phoenix, AZ 85012

ARKANSAS
Worker's Compensation
Commission
625 Marshall Street
Little Rock, AR 72201

CALIFORNIA
State Compensation Insurance Fund
1275 Market Street
San Francisco, CA 94103

COLORADO
Worker's Compensation Sec.
1313 Sherman Street, Rm .314
Denver, CO 80203

CONNECTICUT
Worker's Compensation Commission
1890 Dixwell Avenue
Hamden, CT 06514

DELAWARE
Industrial Accident Board
820 North French Street
Wilmington, DE 19801

DISTRICT OF COLUMBIA
Office of Worker's Compensation
P.O. Box 56098
Washington, DC 20011

FLORIDA
Division of Worker's
Compensation
1321 Executive Center Drive
Tallahassee, FL 32399

GEORGIA Board of Worker's
Compensation
One CNN Center
Atlanta, GA 30303

HAWAII
Disability Compensation Div.
830 Punchbowl Street
Honolulu, Hawaii 96813

IDAHO
Idaho Industrial Commission
317 Main Street
Boise, ID 83720

INDIANA
Industrial Board
100 North Senate Avenue
Indianapolis, IN 46204

KANSAS
Department of Worker's Claims
1270 Louisville Road
Frankfort, KY 40601

MAINE
Worker's Compensation Commission
State House, Room 27
Augusta, ME 04333

MASSACHUSETTS
Industrial Accident Board
600 Washington Street
Boston, MA 02111

MINNESOTA
Worker's Compensation Div.
443 Lafayette Road
St. Paul, MN 55155

MISSOURI
Division of Worker's Compensation
P.O. Box 58
Jefferson City, MO 65102

ILLINOIS
Illinois Industrial Commission
100 West Randolph
Chicago, IL 60611

IOWA
Ind. Commissioner's Office
1000 East Grand Street
Des Moines, IA 50319

LOUISIANA
Office of Worker's
Compensation
P.O. Box 94040
Baton Rouge, LA 70804

MARYLAND
Worker's Compensation
Commission
6 North Liberty Street
Baltimore, MD 21201

MICHIGAN
Bureau of Worker's Disability
P.O. Box 30016
Lansing, MI 48909

MISSISSIPPI
Worker's Compensation
Commission
P.O. Box 5300
Jackson, MS 39216

MONTANA
Division of Worker's
Compensation
5 South Last Chance Gulch
Helena, MT 59604

NEBRASKA
Worker's Compensation Court
P.O. Box 98908
Lincoln, NE 65809

NEVADA
Department of Industrial
Relations
1390 South Curry Street
Carson City, NV 98710

NEW HAMPSHIRE
Worker's Compensation Board
19 Pillsbury Street
Concord, NH 03301

NEW JERSEY
Division of Worker's
Compensation
State Office Building, Rm 381
Trenton, NJ 08625

NEW MEXICO
Worker's Compensation Division
P.O. Box 27198
Albuquerque, NM 87125

NEW YORK
State Insurance Fraud
199 Church Street
New York, NY 10007

NORTH CAROLINA
Industrial Commission
430 North Salisbury Street
Raleigh, NC 27611

NORTH DAKOTA
Worker's Compensation
Bureau 4007 North State St.
Bismark, ND 58501

OHIO
Bureau of Worker's Compensation
246 North High Street
Columbus, OH 43215

OKLAHOMA
Oklahoma Worker's
Compensation Court
1915 North Stiles
Oklahoma City, OK 73105

OREGON
Dept. of Insurance and Finance
Labor and Industries Building
Salem, OR 97310

PENNSYLVANIA
Bureau of Worker's
Compensation
1171 South Cameron Street
Harrisburg, PA 17104

RHODE ISLAND
Dept. of Worker's Compensation
610 Manton Avenue
Providence, RI 02909

SOUTH CAROLINA
Industrial Commission
1615 Marian Street
Columbia, SC 29202

SOUTH DAKOTA
Department of Labor
700 Governors Drive
Pierre, SD 57501

TEXAS
Industrial Accident Board
200 East Riverside Drive
Austin, TX 78704

VERMONT
Dept. of Labor and Industry
120 State Street
Montpelier, VT 05602

WASHINGTON
Dept. of Labor and Industries
General administration Building
Olympia, WA 98504

WISCONSIN
Worker's Compensation Bureau
P.O. Box 7901
Madison, WI 53707

TENNESSEE
Worker's Compensation Div.
501 Union Street
Nashville, TN 37219

UTAH
Worker's Compensation
Fund
P.O. Box 510250
Salt Lake City, UT 84151

VIRGINIA
Industrial Commission
P.O. Box 1794
Richmond, VA 23220

WEST VIRGINIA
Worker's Compensation
Appeal Board 601 Morris St.
Charleston, WV 25301

WYOMING
Worker's Compensation Div.
122 West 25th Street
Cheyenne, WY 82002

STATE BUSINESS-RELATED RECORDS

NOTE: Not all records will be available in each state.

AUTOMOBILE DEALERS:

Licenses are in the name of the business and indicates the ownership, address, license number and principals in the business.

COLLECTION AGENCIES:

Records involve ownership, type of business, location, etc.

CORPORATION RECORDS:

Provides date incorporated, original stock subscribers, amount of authorized stock, resident agent, and current standing with the State. It also provides complete charter information and the nature of the business. Microfiche may also be available which alphabetically lists all individual names indicating the corporation in which he or she is involved.

DEPARTMENT OF GENERAL SERVICES:

(The name of this department may change from jurisdiction to jurisdiction.) This department releases all contracts for State construction as well as most of the other contract for the State. All information is open on bid specifications, requirements for contract, and lists the holders of the contract, as well as a good deal of information concerning the finances of the bidder.

MOTEL, RESTAURANT & LIQUOR STORES:

These licenses cover bars, liquor stores, restaurants, hotels and motels. Information provides holder of liquor license, type of license, tax status and any disciplinary action.

TRUCKERS, TRUCKING FIRMS AND SELF-EMPLOYED TRUCKERS:

This industry is regulated by the federal government. Information may be kept at employer's office and is not required in some states to be submitted to any particular agency.

UNIFORM COMMERCIAL CODE (UCC):

This information may be available through computer access. It includes all financing statements and chattel mortgages. It lists the name of the debtor, creditor and dates of transaction.

STATE HEALTH-RELATED RECORDS

AUTO ACCIDENT REPORTS:

Provides copy of accident reports (in some states this may be available at only a local law-enforcement agency level only). The accident report will list the names and addresses of drivers and witnesses, identify the insurance carrier, and if a person was injured may also identify the hospital, wrecker service, ambulance, etc.

WORKER'S COMPENSATION CLAIM RECORDS:

These records cover reported on-the-job injuries and provides the type of injury, employer and the insurance carrier. A file may be destroyed after 2 years if no further claims are filed. Files of permanent disabilities may be maintained for up to 15 years.

MISCELLANEOUS STATE RECORDS

BOAT REGISTRATION & COMMERCIAL FISHING LICENSE:

All boats registered within the state for either private or commercial use. Names and addresses of present and previous owners. Similar to a vehicle registration.

DRIVER'S LICENSE RECORDS:

Commonly referred to as MVR records. Information may provide the address at the time of issue, physical description, restrictions, date of birth and in some states the social security number. The social security number is the driver's license number in a few states. Driver's history may include traffic violations and accidents for the past 7 years. (States may vary.) Violations and accidents from other states will be included. Status of licenses may indicate subject has a new license in another jurisdiction.

FINANCIAL RESPONSIBILITY:

These records cover persons who do not have insurance at the time of an accident or who did not report the insurance at the time. When insurance is obtained it will provide the name of the carrier, policy number and the terms of the policy. It will also provide the address of the subject at the time proof is given.

MOTOR VEHICLE REGISTRATION RECORDS:

These records cover all automobile, trucks, and mobile homes, providing the date registered, the address at the time of issue, type of vehicle, vehicle I.D. number (VIN), title number and license tag number. A title search may list any co-owners or lien holders, previous owners, dealer, etc.

PRISON AND PAROLE RECORDS:

Anyone who has served a sentence in the State prison system or who has been paroled through the State Pardons, Parole and Probation system will be listed. This does not include a county or city jail or a parole to a county judge's office. Local records may be in other jurisdictions.

STATE FIRE MARSHAL'S RECORDS:

These records contain information on all fires which are investigated by this office.

HOW TO ORDER STATE RECORDS:

IDENTITY:

A subject's full name is usually necessary, including first name, middle initial and last name. A date of birth (DOB) and social security number (SSN) will aid in the correct identity of each individual inquiry. Auto registrations can be checked by name, license tag number, title number or vehicle identification number (VIN).

INFORMATION NEEDED:

Be specific when requesting information. Sometimes other sources are available and may be utilized if the reason for the investigation is known and explained.

E. FEDERAL RECORDS:

1. Interstate Commerce Commission (ICC)

ICC records are available if the person is a truck driver.

2. Census Bureau

Census records are released every 10 years for records 70 years old. These records are available on microfilm at most libraries. These are a must for genealogical purposes and may be accessed by state, family name, or individual name. The latest census record available at this time is for 1920. Census records are available to anyone. Request Form 106-11 from:

> CENSUS BUREAU
> Pittsburgh, Kansas 66762

3. Federal Aviation Authority (FAA)

Enquire as if enquiring about a driver's license. On the left of the envelope write the code: AAC260 . Write to:

> FEDERAL AVIATION AUTHORITY
> Mike Monroney Aero Center
> P.O. Box 25082
> Oklahoma City, OK 73125 (405) 686-7555

4. Social Security Administration

If ever it could be said that we all had a license plate much the same as an automobile, the Social Security Number (SSN) is it! Indeed, the SSN follows us and precedes us in many known ways as well as ways not yet known to us. It is a universal tracking number. All branches of the military service use the SSN as an Identification Number (ID) which appears on the ID Tags (Dog Tags) issued to each service member. In some states the SSN is the Driver's License (DL) number. The SSN appears on all voter registration records which are public. The Internal Revenue Service (IRS) uses the SSN, along with the Federal Tax Number, to identify and record all business and private taxpayers. The SSN appears on health insurance cards carried by millions. The SSN appears on nearly all credit information. There is literally no end to records or files where the SSN appears which in turn means literally no end to the searches which can be made using the SSN.

EXAMPLE: Bill R. and sister lost track of their father after their parents divorced when he and his sister were very young. Forty years passed and the sister was able to obtain the father's SSN. The sister wrote the Social Security Administration requesting she be furnished the current address of their missing father. The Social Security Administration refused to furnish the address to the sister but did pass the letter to the missing father. The missing father contacted the sister and Bill R..

EXAMPLE: Barbara A. was divorced with three children. She met a man whom she grew extremely fond. However she was prudent and contacted U.F.O. and had a background check run on the man using his SSN through a computer data base. The check led to information disclosing that the man was currently married with three children of his own. Based on the information disclosed, using the SSN as an identifier, Barbara A. was able to avoid a potentially damaging or dangerous relationship.

Once the SSN is known, it is possible to obtain accurate information on that number from innumerable sources. A check on SSNs has sometimes disclosed multiple users. The Social Security Administration also maintains a Master Death Record File which can be accessed by U.F.O using an individual or family name. The Social Security Administration will forward, for humanitarian reasons, a letter to a missing person. However, the sender must prove relationship and submit acceptable reasons. Include full name, date of birth, last known address, and SSN if known.

Write to:

> SOCIAL SECURITY ADMINISTRATION
> Director, Locator Service
> 6401 Security Boulevard
> Baltimore, MD 12135

SOCIAL SECURITY NUMBERS

The first three digits of every Social Security Number (SSN) represents the state in which the person resided when the card was issued. Knowing the state of issue may lead to other records such as school records, medical records, voting records, property tax records, census records, marriage records, divorce records, birth and death records, obituaries, cemeteries, church records, newspaper articles and many other records. States are assigned unique three digit area numbers which identify the state of issue. The population of that state determines the number of separate area prefixes. Not all area prefixes have been assigned, for example the current prefixes include:

> 001 - 587
> 589 - 626
> 700 - 728

(Therefore the number 588 is invalid.)

The second two digits are called the group number and may be used to identify a false number or an error. Only certain two digit group numbers have been assigned to a particular state making an invalid two digit group number easy to recognize.

The last four digits of the SSN are miscellaneous serial numbers. Any group of four digits from 0001 through 9999 are valid. Therefore, 0000 is not a valid serial number.

SOCIAL SECURITY PREFIX NUMBERS

The first three numbers of a SSN represents the state of issuance.

001 - 003	New Hampshire	425 - 428	Mississipp
004 - 007	Maine	429 - 432	Arkansas
008 - 009	Vermont	433 - 439	Louisiana
010 - 034	Massachusetts	440 - 448	Oklahoma
035 - 039	Rhode Island	449 - 467	Texas
040 - 049	Connecticut	468 - 477	Minnesota
050 - 134	New York	478 - 485	Iowa
134 - 158	New Jersey	486 - 500	Missouri
159 - 211	Pennsylvania	501 - 502	North Dakota
212 - 220	Maryland	503 - 504	South Dakota
221 - 222	Delaware	505 - 508	Nebraska
223 - 231	Virginia	509 - 515	Kansas
232 - 236	West Virginia	516 - 517	Montana
237 - 246	North Carolina	518 - 519	Idaho
247 - 251	South Carolina	520	Wyoming
252 - 260	Georgia	521 - 524	Colorado
261 - 267	Florida	525	New Mexico
268 - 302	Ohio	526 - 527	Arizona
303 - 317	Indiana	528 - 529	Utah
362 - 386	Illinois	530	Nevada
362 - 386	Michigan	531 - 539	Washington
387 - 399	Wisconsin	540 - 544	Oregon
400 - 407	Kentucky	545 - 573	California
408 - 415	Tennessee	574	Alaska
416 - 424	Alabama	575 - 576	Hawaii

5. **Internal Revenue Service (IRS)**

   The IRS has an office of disclosure in which the next of kin may request a letter be forwarded to a relative.

   EXAMPLE: Ellen R.'s son had been missing for three years. He had run away because of an unhappy childhood. He wanted no contact with his family. His father died and Ellen R. wanted to locate her son. The IRS has an office of "Disclosure" in which the mother may write a letter requesting the letter to her son be forwarded to his current address as reported on his income tax return. Ellen R. wrote the letter. The IRS forwarded the letter. The son contacted his mother.

6. **Postal Service**

   Anyone may enquire by mail, or in person, at the Post Office serving the zip code (if known) of the missing person about the missing person's address.

   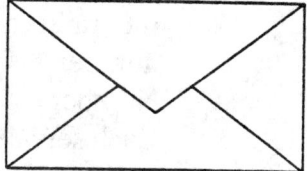

   Information provided by the Post Office:

   > Verify current address
   > Verify forwarding address
   > Verify box holder if box is business

   The Post Office will charge $3.00 to give a person's new forwarding address (if the missing person filled out a change of address). The Post Office will provide the name of the owner and home address of a post office box if it is used for business; not personal. Contacting the carrier for a person who has moved usually provides more information. A personal conversation, rather than a phone call, is more likely to produce results. In rural areas, a mail carrier is more likely to know almost everyone on their respective routes personally. Getting information from rural areas is an art in itself.

TECHNIQUE: Mail a letter to the missing person. Mark the envelop *"Do Not Forward - Address Correction Requested".* The Post Office will return the letter to the sender with the corrected address if the missing person left a forwarding address at the Post Office. If the forwarding address has expired, the envelope will be so marked. If so, the carrier may be able to provide the information.

7. **Military Services (Active Duty and Retired)**

All military services maintain locator activities for both active duty and retired personnel, including National Guard and Reserve Forces. As previously mentioned, the military service identification number is the Social Security Number of the service member. Each service member is also issued an identification card (ID Card) which has its own unique identification number. A service member may be identified through either the SSN or the ID card number. Send the missing person's name, date of birth, Social Security Number, and rank to:

U.S. Army
Worldwide Locator Service
U.S. Army Personnel Service Support Center
Fort Benjamin Harrison, IN 46249
(317) 542-4211

U.S. Air Force
Worldwide Locator
Randolph AFB
San Antonio, TX 78150

U.S. Navy
Navy Locator Service
Navy Annex Building
Washington, D.C. 20370
(202) 694-3155

U.S. Marine Corps
Marine Corps Headquarters Locator Service
Washington, D.C. 20380
(202) 694-1624

U.S. Coast Guard
Coast Guard Locator Service
Room 4502 (enlisted)
Room 420B (commissioned)
2100 2nd Street, SW
Washington, D.C. 20593

Retired Military and Civil Service Personnel
The Office of Personnel Management
1900 E Street SW
Washington, D.C. 20415

Military Records (WWI to present)
General Services Administration
National Personnel Records Center
9700 Page Boulevard
Saint Louis, MO 83232
(512) 652-5775

All states maintain war records. All persons serving in the military service from that state will be recorded. If the missing person is a member of the National Guard of that state, his entire military history will be maintained by that state at the state Department of Military Affairs or equivalent.

As a minimum the military records will show:

- » Enlistments
- » Discharges

WHERE TO WRITE GOVERNMENT LOCATOR SERVICES

The Social Security Administration has one of the largest government databases of names, addresses and dates of births. The Social Security Administration has an office which will forward a letter to a lost family member or someone who is trying to locate a person to give money due them, as from unclaimed property such as an inheritance. This service is offered for humanitarian purposes only. A letter may be sent to the SSA Letter Forwarding Service, Office of Central Records Operations, 300 North Greene Street, Baltimore, MD 21201. The SSA will not furnish the address, only forward a letter in care of the employer who filed the last quarterly earnings report or in care of the last address in which they received Social Security benefits. As in all requests for information you should provide as much identifying information as you know about the missing person such as a full name, date of birth, last known address, social security number, etc. You may enclose another envelope sealed with a personal letter inside the envelope to be forwarded. This envelope may contain a return address from you.

The Internal Revenue Service also provides an Office of Disclosure which will forward a letter for a family member. In order for this letter to be forwarded it is required that you furnish a Social Security number because this is also the taxpayer's identification number. As stated in another chapter, the Social Security number is a universal tracking number capable of tracing a person through records for an entire lifetime. Unfortunately those persons who are deliberately missing rarely use the correct number in order not to be found, therefore making it difficult to track. Check your phone book for the nearest IRS office. They will provide the address of the Office of Disclosure nearest you.

The Veteran's Administration will forward a letter to any veteran who has ever applied for VA benefits or filed a claim. There are approximately five million veterans listed in their files. The regional office of the VA should be listed in your telephone directory under United States Government Offices. When requesting a letter be forwarded through the VA, send an envelope to that address and enclose:

- an unsealed, stamped envelope without your return address and with the subject's name and VA file number or SSN on it;
- a letter to the VA requesting that the letter be forwarded and providing any identifying information you have that would help in locating the subject's records such as a full name, date of birth, approximate dates of military service, a service ID number if known, or any other pertinent information.

You may also have a letter forwarded to a retired federal employee by writing:

Office of Personnel Management
P.O. Box 45
Boyers, PA 16017

8. Private Search Services

There are many private search and information services. These services are private businesses and are available on a fee basis. About 75% of all missing persons can be found using such services. A variety of services are available. U.F.O., INC. offers this service. For more information write to:

U.F.O., INC.
P.O. Box 290333
Nashville, TN 37229-0333

9. Bankruptcy Records

Federal courts handle bankruptcies. These records may be found in the appropriate court and will contain information pertaining to nearly every aspect of the person's life. These records are accessed much the same as in state or county courts and will show:

Assets
Businesses
Creditors
Names
Addresses
Social Security Numbers

EXAMPLE: An attorney asked me to locate Tim D. I was given a name only. I checked to see if Tim might have filed a bankruptcy. I located a bankruptcy and on the public record I was able to obtain his date of birth, social security number, last known address, spouse and employer as well as all the people to whom he owed money. Once I had his last known address, I was able to obtain his forwarding address from the Post Office.

WHERE TO WRITE FOR BANKRUPTCY RECORDS

ALABAMA
United States Bankruptcy Court
500 South 22nd Street
Birmingham, AL 35233

United States Bankruptcy Court
P.O. Box 1248
Montgomery, AL 36192

United States Bankruptcy Court
P.O. Box 2865
Mobile, AL 36652

ALASKA
United States Bankruptcy Court
222 West 7th Avenue
Anchorage, AK 99513

ARKANSAS
United States Bankruptcy Court
P.O. Box 2381
Little Rock, AR 72203

CALIFORNIA
United States Bankruptcy Court
312 North Spring Street
Los Angeles, CA 90012

United States Bankruptcy Court
940 Front Street
San Diego, CA 92189

United States Bankruptcy Court
1130 O Street
Fresno, CA 93721

United States Bankruptcy Court
450 Golden Gate Avenue
San Francisco, CA 94102

United States Bankruptcy Court
Post Office Box 5267
Modesto, CA 95352

COLORADO
United States Bankruptcy Court
1845 Sherman Street
Denver, CO 80203

CONNECTICUT
United States Bankruptcy Court
450 Main Street
Hartford, CT 06103

DELAWARE
United States Bankruptcy Court
844 North King Street
Wilmington, DE 19801

DISTRICT OF COLUMBIA
United States Bankruptcy Court
300 Constitution Avenue, NW
Washington, DC 20001

FLORIDA
United States Bankruptcy Court
51 Southwest 1st Avenue
Miami, FL 33101

United States Bankruptcy Court
299 East Broward Boulevard
Fort Lauderdale, FL 33301

LOUISIANA
United States Bankruptcy Court
500 Camp Street
New Orleans, LA 70130

United States Bankruptcy Court
412 North 4th Street
Baton Rouge, LA 70802

United States Bankruptcy Court
500 Fannin Street
Shreveport, LA 71109

MAINE
United States Bankruptcy Court
156 Federal Way
Portland, ME 04112

MARYLAND
United States Bankruptcy Court
101 West Lombard Street
Baltimore, MD 21201

MASSACHUSETTS
United States Bankruptcy Court
10 Causeway
Boston, MA 02222

MICHIGAN
United States Bankruptcy Court
231 West Lafayette Street
Detroit, MI 48226

United States Bankruptcy Court
P.O. Box 3310
Grand Rapids, MI 49501

MINNESOTA
United States Bankruptcy Court
316 North Robert Street
St. Paul, MN 55101

United States Bankruptcy Court
330 2nd Avenue
Minneapolis, MN 55401

MISSISSIPPI
United States Bankruptcy Court
245 East Capitol Street
Jackson, MS 39201

United States Bankruptcy Court
Post Office Box 369
Biloxi, MS 39533

United States Bankruptcy Court
Post Office Box 867
Aberdeen, MS 39730

MISSOURI
United States Bankruptcy Court
1114 Market Street
St. Louis, MO 63101

United States Bankruptcy Court
811 Grand Avenue
Kansas City, MO 64106

MONTANA
United States Bankruptcy Court
273 Federal Building
Butte, MT 59701

NEBRASKA
United States Bankruptcy Court
Post Office Box 428
Omaha, NB 68101

NEVADA
United States Bankruptcy Court
300 Las Vegas Boulevard
Las Vegas, NV 89101

NEW HAMPSHIRE
United States Bankruptcy Court
275 Chestnut Street
Manchester, NH 03101

NEW JERSEY
United States Bankruptcy Court
15 North 7 Street
Camden, NJ 08102

United States Bankruptcy Court
Post Office Box 515
Trenton, NJ 08603

NEW MEXICO
United States Bankruptcy Court
Post Office Box 546
Albuquerque, NM 87103

NEW YORK
United States Bankruptcy Court
1 Bowling Green
New York NY 10004

United States Bankruptcy Court
75 Clinton Street
Brooklyn, NY 11201

United States Bankruptcy Court
Post Office Box 398
Albany, NY 12201

United States Bankruptcy Court
68 Court Street
Buffalo, NY 14202

United States Bankruptcy Court
100 State Street
Rochester, NY 14614

NORTH CAROLINA
United States Bankruptcy Court
Post Office Box 26100
Greensboro, NC 27420

United States Bankruptcy Court
Post Office Box 2807
Wilson, NC 27894

United States Bankruptcy Court
100 Otis Street
Asheville, NC 28801

NORTH DAKOTA
United States Bankruptcy Court
Post Office Box 1110
Fargo, ND 58107

OHIO
United States Bankruptcy Court
1716 Spielbusch Avenue
Toledo, OH 43624

United States Bankruptcy Court
201 Superior Avenue
Cleveland, OH 44114

United States Bankruptcy Court
2 South Main Street
Akron, OH 44308

United States Bankruptcy Court
9 West Front Street
Youngstown, OH 44501

United States Bankruptcy Court
201 Cleveland Avenue
Canton, OH 44702

United States Bankruptcy Court
85 Marconi Boulevard
Columbus, OH 43215

OKLAHOMA
United States Bankruptcy Court
201 Dean McGee Avenue
Oklahoma City, OK 73102

United States Bankruptcy Court
111 West Fifth Street
Tulsa, OK 74103

United States Bankruptcy Court
Post Office Box 1347
Okmulgee, OK 74447

OREGON
United States Bankruptcy Court
Post Office Box 1335
Eugene, OR 97440

United States Bankruptcy Court
1001 Southwest Fifth Avenue
Portland, OR 97204

PENNSYLVANIA
United States Bankruptcy Court
1602 Liberty Avenue
Pittsburgh, PA 15222

United States Bankruptcy Court
197 South Main Street
Wilkes Barre, PA 18701

United States Bankruptcy Court
601 Market Street
Philadelphia, PA 19106

RHODE ISLAND
United States Bankruptcy Court
380 Westminster Mall
Providence, RI 02903

SOUTH CAROLINA
United States Bankruptcy Court
Post Office Box 1448
Columbia, SC 29202

SOUTH DAKOTA
United States Bankruptcy Court
Post Office Box 5060
Sioux Falls, SD 57115

TENNESSEE
United States Bankruptcy Court
701 Broad Street
Nashville, TN 37203

United States Bankruptcy Court
Post Office Box 2348
Knoxville, TN 37901

United States Bankruptcy Court
969 Madison Avenue
Memphis, TN 38104

TEXAS
United States Bankruptcy Court
1100 Commerce Street
Dallas, TX 75242

United States Bankruptcy Court
211 West Ferguson Street
Tyler, TX 75702

United States Bankruptcy Court
501 West 10th Street
Ft. Worth, TX 76102

United Stated Bankruptcy Court
1205 Texas Avenue
Lubbock, TX 79401

United States Bankruptcy Court
515 Rusk Avenue
Houston, TX 77002

United States Bankruptcy Court
Post Office Box 1439
San Antonio, TX 78295

UTAH
United States Bankruptcy Court
350 South Main Street
Salt Lake City, UT 84101

VERMONT
United States Bankruptcy Court
Post Office Box 6648
Rutland, VT 05702

VIRGINIA
United States Bankruptcy Court
206 North Washington Street
Alexandria, VA 22314

United States Bankruptcy Court
Post Office Box 676
Richmond, VA 23206

United States Bankruptcy Court
600 Granby Street
Norfolk, VA 23510

United States Bankruptcy Court
Post Office Box 497
Newport News, VA 23607

United States Bankruptcy Court
Post Office Box 2390
Roanoke, VA 24010

WASHINGTON
United States Bankruptcy Court
1200 Sixth Avenue
Seattle, WA 98101

United States Bankruptcy Court
Post Office Box 2164
Spokane, WA 99201

WEST VIRGINIA
United States Bankruptcy Court
Post Office Box 3924
Charleston, WV 25301

United States Bankruptcy Court
Post Office Box 70
Wheeling, WV 26003

WISCONSIN
United States Bankruptcy Court
517 West Wisconsin Avenue
Milwaukee, WI 53202

United States Bankruptcy Court
Post Office Box 548
Madison, WI 53701

WYOMING
United States Bankruptcy Court
Post Office Box 1107
Cheyenne, WY 82003

FEDERAL TELEPHONE INFORMATION SOURCES

Congress	House	(202) 225-3121
	Senate	(202) 224-3121
Department of Commerce		(202) 377-2000
Department of Defense	(All Military Branches)	(703) 545-6700
Department of Justice	Inmate Monitoring Service	(202) 307-3036
	Inmate Locate Service	(202) 307-7255
Drug Enforcement Adm.	Drug Registration	(202) 307-7255
Federal Aviation Adm.	Main	(202) 267-3484
	Aircraft Registration	(405) 680-3205
	Pilot Certification	(405) 680-3205
Federal Election Commission		(202) 219-3420
		(800) 424-9530
General Services Administration		(202) 535-0800
Government Printing Office		(202) 512-0000
Interpol (International Child Abduction)		(202) 272-8383
Library of Congress	Main	(202) 707-5000
	National Reference Center	(202) 707-5522
Military Locators (Active)	Air Force	(512) 652-5774
	Navy	(703) 614-3155
	Army	(317) 542-4211
	Marines	(703) 640-3942
Military Personnel Records All Branches		(314) 263-3901
National Archives		(202) 501-5402
National Center for Missing & Exploited Children		(800) 843-5678
National Institute of Standards & Technology		(301) 975-2000
National Ocean & Atmospheric Administration		(301) 443-8330
National Transportation Safety Board		(202) 382-6600
U.S. Coast Guard (locators)	Active	(202) 267-1615
	Reserves	(202) 267-0547
	Retired	(202) 267-4000
U.S. Department of State	Country Desks	(202) 647-4000
U.S. Merchant Marine Locator (U.S. Coast Guard)		(202) 267-0214
U.S. Patent & Trademark Office		(202) 557-5168
Veterans Pension Information		(202) 233-2044
The White House	Office of Agency Liaison	(202) 456-7486

WRITE FOR CATALOGS

Information USA
P.O. Box 15700
Chevy Chase, MD 20815
(301) 657-1200

Superintendent of Documents
U.S. Government Printing Office
North Capital & H Street NW
Washington, DC 20402
(202) 275-2051

Consumer Information Center
P.O. Box 100
Pueblo, CO 81002
(719) 948-3334

Staff Directories
Congressional Government
Judiciary
Mt. Vernon, VA 22121
(703) 765-3400

Washington Researchers
2612 P Street NW
Washington, DC 20007
(202) 333-3499

F. OTHER

1. Financial Records

　a. Credit Bureau

　b. Creditors

　c. Social Security Number

　d. Debtors

　e. Credit Cards

　f. Banks

TECHNIQUE: All banks have a bookkeeping line, or credit line to verify whether a customer has a checking, savings or other account. Some may ask your name and phone number to call you back with the information. Once they verify that John Doe has a savings account, ask "How many digits?" The bank may respond with "5". Then ask "High, Medium or Low?" The bank may respond with "Medium". Therefore you may conclude the account is in the medium 5 digit amount range, or approximately $50,000. (This is one of the ways consumer credit reporting agencies might gather this information.)

2. Relatives

If you say you are working on a family tree or genealogy, relatives may be more cooperative.

3. Employer

Employers may only verify information.

4. Former Employers

Depending on the circumstances, former employer's may or may not give information in addition to verifying employment.

5. **Unions**

   People who belong to unions in one city will probably practice the same trade wherever they go--therefore, will possibly be in the same union in another city.

6. **Schools**

   EXAMPLE: I call a college alumni office looking for Terry G. I am told that this information is not public. I ask if they might just verify the address I already have. They check and tell me he has moved and give me his new address.

7. **Subscriptions**

   Mailing lists may be available.

8. **Churches, Clubs, Associations, and Organizations**

   Many churches and clubs now maintain computerized records. Such organizations maintain at least mailing lists, telephone numbers, employment, and other information about their members. Most churches and clubs, even if not computerized, maintain membership rosters and directories. Talking to members of churches and clubs, especially their clergy or presidents may often gain access to the information desired.

   EXAMPLE: Mark A. retired from his job and moved away. No one heard from him for years. He was a member of the Rotary Club before his retirement. Checking the Rotary Directory lead to his current location.

9. **Salesmen**

   Car, real estate, and insurance salesmen, among others, maintain records of customers in order to provide future service and make additional sales. Many of them have mailing lists to provide a method of staying in touch with their customers through the use of such things as Christmas Card and other similar mailings. The paper trail of the missing person may very well lead to a salesman.

10. Former Spouse

Care should be taken when approaching former spouses because of the emotion associated with divorce and other family problems. However, former spouses usually have records of some kind remaining from the marriage which may be made available depending on the approach and other circumstances.

11. Friends and Associates

As with former spouses, caution is required. Friends and associates may be protective. A "cover story" may be necessary. However, friends and associates know about social life, business associates, interests, hang outs, and other personal data about the missing person. These persons may have some type of records such as addresses or telephone numbers, and in most cases can direct the searcher to places to look for the paper trail.

12. Medical Records

A release or court order may be necessary to gain access to medical records. Insurance records require a medical authorization. Check each state law for individual restrictions.

EXAMPLE: Kelly M. was adopted and wanted to locate her birth mother. She had obtained her mother's name. She also knew her date of birth and the hospital in which she was born. Medical records may be obtained with a medical authorization form signed either by the person or next of kin. Kelly requested her birth records from the hospital where she was born. The records named her mother, gave the mother's address at the time of birth, social worker she was released to, and other information that she used to find her birth mother.

(More on searching for birthparents, siblings and adoptees and others available through U.F.O., Inc. seminars and in my other books written exclusively for adoption searches. Also see Chapter XII.)

G. UTILITIES

1. **Landlord**
2. **Gas Company**
3. **Electric Company**
4. **Telephone Company**
5. **Garbage Service**

All utilities use application forms and usually require deposits when providing services. The information on the application may vary, but there will usually be:

> Name/Address
> Telephone number
> Employer
> Reference/Relative

Both business and government have grown more protective of customer information due to various privacy laws and may not furnish information to the searcher. However, they will usually verify information. Again, skillful questioning is in order.

EXAMPLE: Utility company records may not be public, but the company will verify certain information for particular reasons. For example, the electric, gas or water company may give a church or charity organization information if they think the person they are checking on is being dishonest. If a woman goes to a church to request help in paying her electric bill and she does not really owe for the bill, the electric company wants to let the church know she is not truly needy. Therefore they share the information.

H. LAST KNOWN ADDRESS

The last known address of a missing person may often be known by others and can be found in many places. The missing person may have inadvertently left one or more clues to who might know his forwarding address. The places to look are:

>Neighbors
>Local area merchants
>Landlord
>Real estate agent
>Household members
>Mail carrier
>Friends
>Creditors
>Clubs

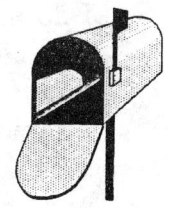

EXAMPLE: Time may be saved by consulting a cross reference directory to locate the oldest neighbor in the neighborhood. The oldest neighbor usually remembers or knows something about nearly everyone in the area.

EXAMPLE: A Private Investigator contacted me recently requesting that I find a family who owned a recording studio in the Nashville area in 1967. The investigator gave me an unusual spelling of the last name. I looked in the 1967 Polk directory for all families with this last name and there were only a few. One man was listed as being a recording engineer. I obtained his address and I looked in a current phone book for this man's name and it was not there. I looked up the address in the current Criss Cross Directory and the family was no longer there. I noted the next door neighbor at this address in 1967 still resided at this location. I contacted this neighbor who kept in touch with the family and gave me the man's Florida address.

TECHNIQUE: I usually look for a neighbor who has lived in the area the longest. If they cannot help, they may give me the name of someone who can. Most older neighbors are very cooperative and helpful. They sometimes want first to know why you are looking for this person. Be very calm and non-threatening. Explain that you are just trying to help someone who was an old friend or relative (genealogy works best). If they think they are going to get their friend or neighbor in trouble they will probably not want to help or become involved, but if they think they are doing a favor or helping this person, they are more likely to be cooperative. I do not recommend misrepresentation, pretext, or obtaining information under false pretense — just realize and be aware that sometimes a direct approach is oftentimes misunderstood and seems threatening with whomever you are talking. I cannot stress enough the importance of being very non-threatening when trying to obtain information from anyone. This is one of my true secrets for successful searching. If you get nothing else from reading this book, remember to be non-threatening when trying to obtain information.

WHERE TO WRITE FOR HOMELESS RECORDS

The Salvation Army operates a locator service for finding homeless persons. It will only help searchers who have a positive motive, primarily those searching for lost family members. The Salvation Army may not tell you where the homeless person is, but may pass on the message that you wish to contact them. The regional addresses for the Salvation Army Missing Persons Services are:

- Eastern U.S.:
  120 W. 14th Street
  New York, NY 10011

- Central U.S.:
  860 N. Dearborn Street
  Chicago, IL 60610

- Southern U.S.:
  1424 N.E. Expressway
  Atlanta, GA 30329

- Western U.S.:
  30840 Hawthorne Boulevard Rancho
  Palos Verdes, CA 90274

The sharp rise in the number of homeless since the late 1970s has led to a plethora of private and local government agencies providing health care and counseling as well as operating soup kitchens and shelters. Many churches, homeless shelters, rescue missions and other non-profit organizations provide services once traditionally provided by the Salvation Army and are located in almost every city. To find appropriate agencies in your locality, look in the local community resources directory at your public library. In New York City, you can look in The Source Book, the Directory of Community Services, or the Directory of Alcoholism Resources and Services. The social service agencies listed in such directories are your most practical means of communicating with the homeless population if the Salvation Army cannot help.

Even homeless people must have some form of identification in case they need medical attention. In order to receive free medical, food, or other service, a homeless person may have to show an identification card of some type. Of course, they may use any name, not necessarily their real names. It is not uncommon for homeless people to change their identities. Homeless people oftentimes want to forget an unhappy, painful past, therefore they do not wish to be called the name that brings these memories.

Since homeless people do not work or pay taxes, there are no paper trails to follow. They may have a birth certificate, a social security number, a voter registration card, but the trails may not lead anywhere. Unless they pay taxes, use credit, have a bank account or work, the only trail that may exist on paper is medical and that is not public. Even a medical record may be under a false name. In some states the only form of identification that is required for the best in free medical care is only a voter registration card. To obtain this card one may only provide an envelope with a name and address, a false birth certificate, a false driver's license, a false social security number. Voter registration records are not necessarily cross-referenced, nor is information verified, therefore a voter may be registered in numerous locations. An election could easily be thrown by homeless people registering under many identities.

Not all homeless people are truly needy. One man actually lives in an apartment with his girlfriend, but tells the welfare office he lives in his car so he can draw $120.00 per month for one year with no verification. He can leave that city and come to another city, have only a voter's registration card for identification and receive free medical care. For $68.00 he may buy a round-trip bus ticket and travel the U.S. collecting checks along the way. Several states will pay several hundred dollars to get a homeless person to leave. This type of fraud is practically untraceable because no positive identification is required. A photo identification card, like a credit card with fingerprints and verified information will probably one day track the steps of the homeless.

A homeless person, or anyone else for that matter, can stand on a busy street corner with a sign reading "Hungry, will work for food" and easily make $100.00 per day. This money is used for alcohol, cigarettes and drugs in many cases. Food is available, therefore they are not truly hungry. If you stand back and watch, they may even have a car parked nearby, or someone may pick them up a block or so away. I have even observed handicapped people switching places in a wheelchair.

CHAPTER IV - SEARCHING

Your objective is to find the missing person. In order to do that, it is necessary to find an address through a record or another person. That is the end upon which to focus the search. It is necessary to retain a certain skepticism, especially when receiving information from a person. Information received from another person may be faulty or deliberately misleading. Check and double check all information. Rely on your intuition, it is usually correct.

DATABASES

There is a nearly unlimited source of information available in the form of commercial databases. National and state searches are done via these databases. Should you, as a searcher, decide to use a Private Investigator or search firm, I would recommend that you employ a firm who  has the in-house capability to do a nationwide computer database search. It is possible to search nationwide with a name only. Death record searches are also available with a name only or all deaths since 1962. These records are invaluable to a searcher working on genealogy.

U.F.O., Inc.
P.O. Box 290333
Nashville, TN 37229-0333

A sampling of the types of searches available through U.F.O., INC.'s computer, is:

- consumer credit information from over 1000 credit reporting agencies containing over 350 million files
- nationwide surname searches
- social security number tracing and verification for name and address identification, over 300 million files

- address identification and updates – including information on social security numbers, employer information, present and previous addresses, over 250 million files
- nationwide cross referencing for names, phone numbers and addresses, including searches for identifying neighbor's addresses and phone numbers with over 92 million files
- nationwide driving record information – providing validity of license, moving violations, arrests, and reported addresses assigned to the driver's license number (DL #) you provide
- nationwide driver's license number search - provided from only the subject's name, date of birth, and the state you wish searched
- nationwide alpha name search - provided from the subject's name, last known address or state which you want searched to determine their driver's license number, record and vehicle ownership
- nationwide license plate identification search, provided from any plate/tag number you request and the state to be searched, to determine the ownership of the vehicle and all addresses assigned to that plate number and it's vehicle identification number (VIN)
- nationwide (VIN) search, provided from the VIN you provide and the state to be searched, to determine ownership of the vehicle and it's plate/tag number
- commercial business profiles - describing a business's credit history, profit and loss history, length of business, type of business, officers, banking and loan references, payment trends, number of employees, sales volume etc.
- nationwide criminal history record searches - providing any criminal convictions from the county or state you wish searched, or any federal criminal convictions at the county or state level

- nationwide worker compensation claim searches on your subject by state, to determine any claims filed and the types of claims filed
- nationwide business cross referencing by business phone number, name, and address information, containing over 8 million files
- Federal Aviation Administration searches by tail number or pilot name for owner registration information
- death record searches through the Social Security Administration's Master Death Record File, over 41 million records

In an attempt to satisfy client need for expedient, accurate and efficient information retrieval, certain databases are accessible instantly. Those search services that are interactive, immediate response databases which have instant turnaround time are:

- consumer credit reports
- commercial business reports
- social security number tracing
- address identification and updates
- name, address, and phone number cross referencing
- neighbor look-up by name, address and phone number

These searches are identified as interactive because the databases containing this information are accessed and instantly transmitted to the U.F.O. computer.

Other searches may require a greater turnaround time because not every source for the information is computerized or the information requires special releases because of the confidentiality of the information. Those searches normally requiring a 1 to 7 business day turnaround time are:

- criminal record searches
- driving record searches

- plate/tag and VIN searches
- worker compensation claims
- business cross referencing
- FAA searches

NATIONAL CREDIT INFORMATION NETWORK

THE #1 SOURCE OF INFORMATION!
LIMITED SPECIAL OFFER $795.00

In order to obtain information through the #1 InformationSource, you must be a business or company with a legitimate* need for credit information. An onsight inspection will be made of your office and a background check will be conducted to verify all information before anyone is approved and allowed access to use this source.
*You must qualify under the Fair Credit Reporting Act in order to obtain credit information.

WHAT EQUIPMENT IS NECESSARY TO ACCESS THIS DATABASE?
A computer with a modem. (PCPLUS/2400 BAUD - 9600 BAUD)

WHAT INFORMATION IS AVAILABLE THRU THIS DATABASE?

Consumer Credit Reports - over 350 million files

Social Security number tracing and verification - over 300 million files

Address identification and updates - over 250 million files

Nationwide Kris-Cross for cross referencing names, phone numbers, addresses, neighbors - over 92 million files

Nationwide driving record information

Nationwide driver's license number search

Nationwide license plate identification

Nationwide name search

Nationwide criminal history record searches

Nationwide worker's compensation claims

Nationwide business cross referencing

Federal Aviation Administration searches - pilots/aircraft

Death Records - over 41 million files

TRY BEFORE YOU BUY!
FREE DEMONSTRATION OF THIS DATABASE: CALL (513) 521-4420
(PASSWORD: DEMO53)
FOR ADDITIONAL INFORMATION:
U.F.O., INC. / P.O. Box 290333 / Nashville, TN 37229-0333
(615) 366-5181 FAX: (615) 366-5481

CHAPTER V - THE PRIVACY ACT

The Privacy Act, passed by Congress in 1974, establishes certain controls over what personal information is collected by the federal government and how it is used. The Act guarantees three primary rights:

1. the right to see records about yourself, subject to the Privacy Act's exemptions

2. the right to amend that record if it is inaccurate, irrelevant, untimely, or incomplete

3. the right to sue the government for violations of the statute, including permitting others to see your records, unless specifically permitted by the Act

The Privacy Act applies only to documents about individuals maintained by agencies in the executive branch of the federal government. It applies to these records only if they are in a "system" of records, which means they are retrieved by an individual's name, social security number, or some other personal identifier.

The Privacy Act does not apply to records held by Congress, the courts, local governments or private organizations (except for the limitation upon the use of the social security account number, which does not apply to state and local governments).

There are ten exemptions to the Privacy Act under which an agency can withhold certain kinds of information from you. Examples of exempt records are those containing classified information on national security or those concerning criminal investigations. Another exemption is that which protects the identity of a confidential source. The ten exemptions are set out in the Act.

The Act is published in its entirety in both the U.S. Government Manual and the U.S. Code. These publications can be found in most public and school libraries. You may order a copy the Privacy Act of 1974, Public Law 93-579, from:

The Superintendent of Documents:
U.S. Government Printing Office
Washington, D.C. 20402

Enclose $2.50 and specify stock number 022-003-90866-8.

CHAPTER VI - The Freedom of Information Act (FOIA)

The FOIA provides access to all federal agency records (or portions of those records) except those which are protected from release by nine specific exemptions. The exemptions cover such material as:

- Classified national defense and foreign relations information
- Internal agency personnel rules and practices
- Material prohibited from disclosure by another law
- Trade secrets and other confidential business information
- Certain inter or intra agency communications
- Personnel, medical and other files involving personal privacy
- Certain investigatory records compiled for law enforcement purposes
- Matters relating to the management of financial institutions
- Geological information on oil wells

The FOIA does not apply to Congress or the courts, nor does it apply to the records of state and local governments. However, most states have their own FOIA-type laws. You may request information about a state's law by writing the attorney general of that state.

The FOIA does not require a private organization or business to release any information directly to the public, whether it has been submitted to the government or not.

Under the FOIA, you may request and receive a copy of any record that is in an agency's official files and is not covered by one of the exemptions.

An agency may charge only the cost of searching for the materials.

Short Guide to the Freedom of Information Act may be purchased from:

>The Superintendent of Documents
>U.S. Government Printing Office
>Washington D.C. 20402

CHAPTER VII - The Freedom of Information Act and The Privacy Act Compared

Both the FOIA and the Privacy Act give people the right of access to records held by agencies of the federal government. The FOIA's access rights are given to "any person", but the Privacy Act's access rights are only for the individual who is the subject of the records sought. The FOIA applies to all records of federal agencies; the Privacy Act applies only to federal agency records in "systems of records" which can be retrieved by the use of a name or personal identifier and contain information about an individual. If you request records about yourself under both laws, federal agencies may withhold the records from you only to the extent the records are exempt under both laws.

If the information you want pertains to the activities of federal agencies or of another person, you should make your request under the FOIA, which covers all agency records. If the information you want is about yourself and you wish to avoid possible search fees, you should make the request under the Privacy Act, which covers most records of agencies that pertain to individuals.

The FOIA contains a very important provision concerning personal privacy: Exemption 6 protects you from others who may seek information about you, but it also may block you if you seek information about others. Exemption 6 permits an agency to withhold information about individuals if disclosing it would be a "clearly unwarranted invasion of personal privacy". This includes, for example, almost all of the information in medical files and much of the information in personnel files. Exemption 6 cannot be used to deny you information about yourself, only to deny you information about other persons.

Release of information about an individual is considered an invasion of privacy if he or she could reasonably object because of its intimacy or its possible adverse effects upon himself or herself or family. Such information is not protected by Exemption 6 if the injury to the individual is outweighed by a public interest favoring disclosure.

CHAPTER VIII - CREDIT CARD COMPANIES

Credit card companies may provide useable information. The major companies are:

AMERICAN EXPRESS
1200 Concord Pike
Wilmington, DE 18803

CARTE BLANCHE
3460 Wilshire Boulevard
Los Angeles, CA 90010

DINER'S CLUB
10 Columbus Circle
New York, NY 10020

MASTERCARD
1 Custom House
Wilmington, DE 19899

VISA INTERNATIONAL
P.O. Box 8999
San Francisco, CA 94128
(800) 336-8472
Customer Service
New Castle, DE
(800) 241-7990

Information regarding anyone holding a credit card from one of these companies is generally available only to the cardholder. Information about the credit card will show on a credit check. The balance, card number, age, and all information contained on the application for the card will be reflected. When contacting a credit card company directly use the same technique as when talking to a bank. Ask for verification. When verifying information it is best to contact the bank from which the card was issued.

CHAPTER IX - THE FAIR CREDIT REPORTING ACT

Public Law 91-508, Title VI

TITLE VI-PROVISIONS RELATING TO CREDIT REPORTING AGENCIES

AMENDMENT OF CONSUMER CREDIT PROTECTION ACT

SEC.601. The Consumer Credit Protection Act is amended by adding at the end thereof the following new title:

"TITLE VI-CONSUMER CREDIT REPORTING"

"Sec.
"601. Short title.
"602. Findings and purpose.
"603. Definitions and rules of construction.
"604. Permissible purposes of reports.
"605. Obsolete information.
"606. Disclosures to governmental agencies.
"609. Disclosure to consumers.
"610. Conditions of disclosure to consumers.
"611. Procedure in case of disputed accuracy.
"612. Charges for certain disclosures.
"613. Public record information for employment purposes.
"614. Restrictions on investigative consumer reports.
"615. Requirements on users of consumer reports.
"616. Civil liability for willful noncompliance.
"617. Civil liability for negligent noncompliance.
"618. Jurisdiction of courts; limitation of actions.
"619. Obtaining information under false pretenses.
"620. Unauthorized disclosures by officers or employees.
"621. Administrative enforcement.
"622. Relation to State laws.

"601. Short title.

"This title may be cited as the Fair Credit Reporting Act."

"602. Findings and purpose.

"(a) The Congress makes the following findings:

"(1) The banking system is dependent upon fair and accurate credit reporting. Inaccurate credit reports directly impair the efficiency of the banking system, and unfair credit reporting methods undermine the public confidence which is essential to the continued functioning of the banking system.

"(2) An elaborate mechanism has been developed for investigating and evaluating the credit worthiness, credit standing, credit capacity, character, and general reputation of consumers.

"(3) Consumer reporting agencies have assumed a vital role in assembling and evaluating consumer credit and other information on consumers.

"(4) There is a need to insure that consumer reporting agencies exercise their grave responsibilities with fairness, impartiality, and a respect for the consumer's right to privacy.

"(c) It is the purpose of this title to require that consumer reporting agencies adopt reasonable procedures for meeting the needs of commerce for consumer credit, personnel, insurance, and other information in a manner which is fair and equitable to the consumer, with regard to the confidentiality, accuracy, relevancy, and proper utilization of such information in accordance with the requirements of this title."

"603. Definitions and rules of construction.

"(a) Definitions and rules of construction set forth in this section are applicable for the purposes of this title.

"(b) The term 'person' means any individual, partnership, corporation, trust, estate, cooperative, association, government or governmental subdivision or agency, or other entity.

"(c) The term 'consumer' means an individual.

"(d) The term 'consumer report' means any written, oral, or other communication of any information by a consumer reporting agency bearing on a consumer's credit worthiness, credit standing, credit capacity, character, general reputation, personal characteristics, or mode of living which is used or expected to be used or collected in whole or in part for the purpose of serving asa factor in establishing the consumer's eligibility for (1) credit or insurance to be used primarily for personal, family, or household purposes, or (2) employment purposes, or (3) other purposes authorized under section "604. The term does not include (a) any report containing information solely as to transactions or experiences between the consumer and the person making the report: (b) any authorization or approval of a specific extension of credit directly or indirectly by the issuer of a credit card or similar device; or (c) any report in which a person who has been requested by a third party advises the consumer of the name and address of the person to whom the request was made and such person makes the disclosures to the consumer required under section "615.

"(e) The term 'investigative consumer report' means a consumer report or portion thereof in which information on a consumer's character, general reputation, personal characteristics, or mode of living is obtained through personal interviews with neighbors, friends, or associates of the consumer reported on or with others with whom he is acquainted or who may have knowledge concerning any such items of information. However, such information shall not include specific factual information on a consumer or from a consumer reporting agency when such information was obtained directly from a creditor of the consumer or from the consumer.

"(f) The term 'consumer reporting agency' means any person which, for monetary fees, does or on a cooperative nonprofit basis, regularly engages in whole or in part in the practice of assembling or evaluating consumer credit information or other information on consumers for the purpose of furnishing consumer reports to third parties, and which uses any means or facility of interstate commerce for the purpose of preparing or furnishing consumer reports.

"(g) The term 'file', when used in connection with information on any consumer, means all of the information on that consumer recorded and retained by a consumer reporting agency regardless of how the information is stored.

"(h) The term 'employment purposes' when used in connection with a consumer report means a report used for the purpose of evaluating a consumer for employment, promotion, reassignment or retention as an employee.

"(i) The term 'medical information' means information or records obtained, with the consent of the individual to whom it relates, from licensed physicians or medical practitioners, hospitals, clinics, or other medical or medically related facilities."

"604. Permissible purposes of reports.

"A consumer reporting agency may furnish a consumer report under the following circumstances and no other:

"(a) In response to the order of a court having jurisdiction to issue such an order.

"(b) In accordance with the written instructions of the consumer to whom it relates.

"(c) To a person which it has reason to believe-

"(1) intends to use the information in connection with a credit transaction involving the consumer on whom the information is to be furnished and involving the extension of credit to, or review or collection of an account of the consumer; or

"(2) intends to use the information for employment purposes; or

"(3) intends to use the information in connection with the underwriting of insurance involving the consumer; or

"(4) intends to use the information in connection with a determination of the consumer's eligibility for a license or other benefit granted by a governmental instrumentality required by law to consider an applicant's financial responsibility or status; or

"(5) otherwise has a legitimate business need for the information in connection with a business transaction involving the consumer."

"605. Obsolete information.

"(a) Except as authorized under subsection (b), no consumer reporting agency may make any consumer report containing any of the following items of information:

"(1) Cases under title 11 of the United States Code, or under the Bankruptcy Act that, from the date of entry of the order for relief or the date of adjudication, as the case may be, antedate the report by more than 10 years.

"(2) Suits and judgments which, from date of entry, antedate the report by more than seven years or until the governing statute of limitations has expired, whichever is the longer period.

"(3) Paid tax liens which, from date of payment, antedate the report by more than seven years.

"(4) Accounts placed for collection or charged to profit and loss which antedate the report by more than seven years.

"(5) Records of arrest, indictment, or conviction of crime which, from date of disposition, release, on parole, antedate the report by more than seven years.

"(6) Any other adverse item of information which antedates the report by more than seven years.

"(b) The provisions of subsection (a) are not applicable in the case of any consumer credit report to be used in connection with-

"(1) a credit transaction involving, or which may reasonably be expected to involve, a principal amount of $50,000 or more; or

"(2) the underwriting of life insurance involving, or which may reasonably be expected to involve, a face amount of $50,000 or more; or

"(3) the employment of any individual at an annual salary which equals, or which may be reasonable be expected to equal $20,000, or more."

"606. Disclosure of investigative consumer reports.

"(a) A person may not procure or cause to be prepared an investigative consumer report on any consumer unless—

"(1) it is clearly and accurately disclosed to the consumer than an investigative consumer report including information as to his character, general reputation, personal characteristics, and mode of living, whichever are applicable, may be made, and such disclosure (a) is made in a writing mailed, or otherwise delivered, to the consumer, not later than three days after the date on which the report was first requested, and (b) includes a statement informing the consumer of his right to request the additional disclosures provided for under subsection (b) of this section; or

"(2) the report is to be used for employment purposes for which the consumer has not specifically applied.

"(b) Any person who procures or causes to be prepared an investigative consumer report on any consumer shall, upon written request made by the consumer within a reasonable period of time after receipt by him of the disclosure required by subsection (a)(1), shall make a complete and accurate disclosure of the nature and scope of the investigation requested. This disclosure shall be made in a writing mailed, or otherwise delivered, to the consumer not later than five days after the date on which the request for such disclosure was received from the consumer or such report was first requested, whichever is the later.

"(c) No person may be held liable for any violation of subsection (a) or (b) of this section if he shows by a preponderance of the evidence that at the time of the violation he maintained reasonable procedures to assure compliance with subsection (a) or (b)."

"607. Compliance procedures.

"(a) Every consumer reporting agency shall maintain reasonable procedures designed to avoid violations of Section 605 and to limit the furnishing of consumer reports to the purposes listed under section 604. These procedures shall require that prospective users of the information identify themselves, certify the purposes for which the information is sought, and certify that the information will be used for no other purpose. Every consumer reporting agency shall make a reasonable effort to verify the identity of a new prospective user and the uses certified by such prospective user prior to furnishing such user a consumer report. No consumer reporting agency may furnish a consumer report to any person if it has reasonable grounds for believing that the consumer report will not be used for a purpose listed in section 604.

"(b) Whenever a consumer reporting agency prepares a consumer report it shall follow reasonable procedures to assure maximum possible accuracy of the information concerning the individual about whom the report relates."

"608. Disclosures to governmental agencies.

"Notwithstanding the provisions of section 604, a consumer reporting agency may furnish identifying information respecting any consumer, limited to his name, address, former addresses, places of employment, or former places of employment, to a governmental agency."

"609. Disclosures to consumers.

"(a) Every consumer reporting agency shall upon request and proper identification of any consumer, clearly and accurately disclose to the consumer:

"(1) The nature and substance of all information (except medical information) in its files on the consumer at the time of the request.

"(2) The sources of the information; except that the sources of information acquired solely for use in preparing an investigative consumer report and actually used for no other purpose need not be disclosed: provided, that in the event an action is brought under this title, such sources shall be available to the plaintiff under appropriate discovery procedures in the court in which the action is brought.

"(3) The recipients of any consumer report on the consumer which it has furnished

[a] for employment purposes within the two-year period preceding the request, and

[b] for any other purpose within the six-month period preceding the request.

"(b) The requirements of subsection a respecting the disclosure of sources of information and the recipients of consumer reports do not apply to information received or consumer reports furnished prior to the effective date of this title except to the extent that the matter involved is contained in the files of the consumer reporting agency on that date."

"610. Conditions of disclosure to consumers.

"(a) A consumer reporting agency shall make the disclosures required under section 609 during normal business hours and on reasonable notice.

"(b) The disclosures required under section 609 shall be made to the consumer

"(1) in person if he appears in person and furnishes proper identification: or

"(2) by telephone if he has made a written request, with proper identification, for telephone disclosure and the toll charge, if any, for the telephone call is prepaid by or charged directly to the consumer.

"(c) Any consumer reporting agency shall provide trained personnel to explain to the consumer any information furnished to him pursuant to section 609.

"(d) The consumer shall be permitted to be accompanied by one other person of his choosing, who shall furnish reasonable identification. A consumer reporting agency may require the consumer to furnish a written statement granting permission to the consumer reporting agency to discuss the consumer's file in such person's presence.

"(e) Except as provided in sections 616 and 617, no consumer may bring any action or proceeding in the nature of defamation, invasion of privacy, or negligence with respect to the reporting of information against any consumer reporting agency, any user of information, or any person who furnishes information to a consumer reporting agency, based on information disclosed pursuant to section 609, 610, or 615, except as to false information furnished with malice or willful intent to injure such consumer."

"611. Procedure in case of disputed accuracy.

"(a) If the completeness or accuracy of any item of information contained in his file is disputed by a consumer, and such dispute is directly conveyed to the consumer reporting agency by the consumer, the consumer reporting agency shall within a reasonable period of time re-investigate and record the current status of that information unless it has reasonable grounds to believe that the dispute by the consumer is frivolous or irrelevant. If after such re-investigation such information is found to be inaccurate or can no longer be verified, the consumer reporting agency shall promptly delete such information. The presence of contradictory information in the consumer's file does not in and of itself constitute reasonable grounds for believing the dispute is frivolous or irrelevant.

"(b) If the reinvestigation does not resolve the dispute, the consumer may file a brief statement setting forth the nature of the dispute. The consumer reporting agency may limit such statements to not more than one hundred words if it provides the consumer with assistance in writing a clear summary of the dispute.

"(c) Whenever a statement of a dispute is filed, unless there is reasonable grounds to believe that it is frivolous or irrelevant, the consumer reporting agency shall, in any subsequent consumer report containing the information in question, clearly note that it is disputed by the consumer and provide either the consumer's statement or a clear and accurate codification or summary thereof.

"(d) Following any deletion of information which is found to be inaccurate or whose accuracy can no longer be verified or any notation as to disputed information, the consumer reporting agency shall, at the request of the consumer, furnish notification that the item has been deleted or the statement, codification or summary pursuant to subsection (b) or (c) to any person specifically designated by the consumer who has within two years prior thereto received a consumer report for employment purposes, or within six months prior thereto received a consumer report for any other purpose, which contained the deleted or disputed information. The consumer reporting agency shall clearly and conspicuously disclose to the consumer his rights to make such a request. Such disclosure shall be made at or prior to the time the information is deleted or the consumer's statement regarding the disputed information is received."

"612. Charges for certain disclosures.

"A consumer reporting agency shall make all disclosures pursuant to section 609 and furnish all consumer reports pursuant to section 611(d) without charge to the consumer if, within thirty days after receipt by such consumer of a notification pursuant to section 615 or notification from a debt collection agency affiliated with such consumer reporting agency stating that the consumer's credit rating may be or has been adversely affected, the consumer makes a request under section 609 or 611(d). Otherwise, the consumer reporting agency may impose a reasonable charge on the consumer for making disclosure to such consumer pursuant to section 609, the charge for which shall be indicated to the consumer prior to making disclosure; and for furnishing notifications, statements, summaries, or codification to person designated by the consumer pursuant to section 611(d), the charge for which shall be indicated to the consumer prior to furnishing such information and shall not exceed the charge that the consumer reporting agency would impose on each designated recipient for a consumer report except that no charge may be made for notifying such persons of the deletion of information which is found to be inaccurate or which can no longer be verified."

"613. Public record information for employment purposes.

"A consumer reporting agency which furnishes a consumer report for employment purposes and which for that purpose compiles and reports items of information on consumers which are matters of public record and are likely to have an adverse effect upon a consumer's ability to obtain employment shall:

"(a) at the time such public record information is reported to the user of such consumer report, notify the consumer of the fact that public record information is being reported by the consumer reporting agency, together with the name and address of the person to whom such information is being reported; or

"(b) maintain strict procedures designed to insure that whenever public record information which is likely to have an adverse effect on a consumer's ability to obtain employment is reported it is complete and up to date. For purposes of this paragraph, items of public record relating to arrests, indictments, convictions, suits, tax liens, and outstanding judgements shall be considered up to date if the current public record status of the item at the time of the report is reported."

"614. Restrictions on investigative consumer reports.

"Whenever a consumer reporting agency prepares an investigative consumer report, no adverse information in the consumer report (other than information which is a matter of public record) may be included in a subsequent consumer report unless such adverse information has been verified in the process of making such subsequent consumer report, or the adverse information was received within the three-month period preceding the date the subsequent report is furnished."

"615. Requirements on users of consumer reports.

"(a) Whenever credit or insurance for personal, family, or household purposes, or employment involving a consumer is denied or the charge for such credit or insurance is increased either wholly or partly because of information contained in a consumer report from a consumer reporting agency, the user of the consumer report shall so advise the consumer against whom such adverse action has been taken and supply the name and address of the consumer reporting agency making the report.

"(b) Whenever credit for personal, family, or household purposes involving a consumer is denied or the charge for such credit is increased either wholly or partly because of information obtained from a person other than a consumer reporting agency bearing upon the consumer's credit worthiness, credit standing, credit capacity, character, general reputation, personal characteristics, or mode of living, the user of such information shall, within a reasonable period of time, upon the consumer's written request for the reasons for such adverse action received within sixty days after learning of such adverse action, disclose the nature of the information to the consumer. The user of such information shall clearly and accurately disclose to the consumer his right to make such written request at the time such adverse action is communicated to the consumer.

"(c) No person shall be held liable for any violation of this section if he shows by a preponderance of the evidence that at the time of the alleged violation he maintained reasonable procedures to assure compliance with the provisions of subsections (a) and(b)."

"616. Civil liability for willful noncompliance.

"Any consumer reporting agency or user of information which willfully fails to comply with any requirement imposed under this title with respect to any consumer is liable to that consumer in an amount equal to the sum of:

"(a) any actual damages sustained by the consumer as a result of the failure;

"(b) such amount of punitive damages as the court may allow and

"(c) in the case of any successful action to enforce any liability under this section, the costs of the action together with reasonable attorney's fees as determined by the court.

"617. Civil liability for negligent noncompliance.

"Any consumer reporting agency or user of information which is negligent in failing to comply with any requirement imposed under this title with respect to any consumer is liable to that consumer in an amount equal to the sum of:

"(a) any actual damages sustained by the consumer asa result of the failure;

"(b) in the case of any successful action to enforce any liability under this section, the costs of the action together with reasonable attorney's fees as determined by the court."

"618. Jurisdiction of courts limitation of actions.

"An action to enforce any liability created under this title maybe brought in any appropriate United States district court without regard to the amount in controversy, or in any other court of competent jurisdiction, within two years from the date on which the liability arises, except that where a defendant has materially and willfully misrepresented any information required under this title to be disclosed to an individual and the information so misrepresented is material to the establishment of the defendant's liability to that individual under this title, the action may be brought at any time within two years after discovery by the individual of the misrepresentation."

"619. Obtaining information under false pretenses.

"Any person who knowingly and willfully obtains information on a consumer from a consumer reporting agency under false pretenses shall be fined not more than $5,000 or imprisoned not more than one year, or both."

"620. Unauthorized disclosures by officers or employees.

"Any officer or employee of a consumer reporting agency who knowingly and willfully provides information concerning an individual from the agency's files to a person not authorized to receive that information shall be fined not more than $5,000 or imprisoned not more than one year, or both."

"621. Administrative enforcement.

"(a) Compliance with the requirements imposed under this title shall be enforced under the Federal Trade Commission Act by the Federal Trade Commission with respect to consumer reporting agencies and all other persons subject thereto, except to the extent that enforcement of the requirements imposed under this title is specifically committed to some other government agency under subsection (b) hereof. For the purpose of the exercise by the Federal Trade Commission of its functions and powers under the Federal Trade Commission Act, a violation of any requirement or prohibition imposed under this title shall constitute an unfair or deceptive act or practice in commerce in violation of section 5(a) of the Federal Trade Commission Act and shall be subject to enforcement by the Federal Trade Commission under section 5(b) thereof with respect to any consumer reporting agency or person subject to enforcement by the Federal Trade Commission pursuant to this subsection, irrespective of whether that person is engaged in commerce or meets any other jurisdictional tests in the Federal Trade Commission Act. The Federal Trade Commission shall have such procedural investigative, and enforcement powers, including the power to issue procedural rules in enforcing compliance with the requirements imposed under this title and to require the filing of reports, the production of documents, and the appearance of witnesses as though the applicable terms and conditions of the Federal Trade Commission Act were part of this title. Any person violating any of the provisions of this title shall be subject to the penalties and entitled to the privileges and immunities provided in the Federal Trade Commission Act as though the applicable terms and provisions thereof were part of this title."

"(b) Compliance with the requirements imposed under this title with respect to consumer reporting agencies and persons whose consumer reports from such agencies shall be enforced under:

"(1) section 8 of the Federal Deposit Insurance Act, in the case of:

[a] national banks, by the Comptroller of the Currency;

[b] member banks of the Federal Reserve System (other than national banks), by the Federal Reserve Board; and

[c] banks insured by the Federal Deposit Insurance Corporation (other than members of the Federal Reserve System), by the Board of Directors of the Federal Deposit Insurance Corporation.

"(2) section 5 (d) of the Home Owners Loan Act of 1933, section 407 of the National Housing Act, and sections 6 (i) and 17 of the Federal Home Loan Bank Act, by the Federal Home Loan Bank Board (acting directly or through the Federal Savings and Loan Insurance Corporation), in the case of any institution subject to any of those provisions;

"(3) the Federal Credit Union Act, by the Administrator of the National Credit Union Administration with respect to any Federal credit union;

"(4) the Acts to regulate commerce, by the Interstate Commerce Commission with respect to any common carrier subject to those Acts;

"(5) the Federal Aviation Act of 1958, by the Civil Aeronautics Board with respect to any air carrier or foreign air carrier subject to that Act: and

"(6) the Packers and Stockyards Act, 1921 (except as provided in section 406 of that Act), by the Secretary of Agriculture with respect to any activities subject to that Act.

"(c) For the purpose of the exercise by any agency referred to in subsection (b) of its powers under any Act referred to in that subsection, a violation of any requirement imposed under this title shall be deemed to be a violation of a requirement imposed under that Act. In addition to its powers under any provision of law specifically referred to in subsection (b), each of the agencies referred to in that subsection may exercise, for the purpose of enforcing compliance with any requirement imposed under this title any other authority conferred on it by law."

"622. Relation to State laws.

"This title does not annul, alter, affect, or exempt any person subject to the provisions of this title from complying with the laws of any State with respect to the collection, distribution, or use of any information on consumers, except to the extent that those laws are inconsistent with any provision of this title, and then only to the extent of the inconsistency."

CHAPTER X
WHERE TO WRITE FOR VITAL RECORDS

An official certificate of every birth, death, marriage, and divorce should be on file in the locality where the event occurred. The Federal Government does not maintain files of these records. These records are filed permanently either in a state vital statistics office or in a city, county, or other local office.

MARRIAGE AND DIVORCE RECORDS

When requesting marriage or divorce records provide as much information as possible:

1. Full names of both parties.
2. Month, day, and year of marriage or divorce.
3. City, town, county and state of marriage or divorce.
4. State purpose of request.
5. State your relationship to persons whose record is being requested.

To obtain a certified copy of any certificate, it is suggested that you first write or call the vital statistics office in the state or area concerned to request a form and the charges involved. Be sure to include a self-addressed stamped envelope.

Certificate of Marriage
Certificate of Birth
Certificate of Adoption
Certificate of Graduation

ALABAMA	Center for Health Statistics State Department of Public Health 434 Monroe Street Montgomery, AL 36130-1701
ALASKA	Department of Health and Social Services Bureau of Vital Statistics P.O. Box H-02G Juneau, AK 99811-0675
ARIZONA	Arizona Department of Health Services Vital Records Section P.O. Box 3887 Phoenix, AZ 85030
ARKANSAS	Division of Vital Records 4815 West Markham Street Little Rock, AR 72201
CALIFORNIA	Vital Statistics Section Department of Health Services 410 N Street Sacramento, CA 95814
COLORADO	Vital Records Section Colorado Department of Health 4210 East 11th Avenue Denver, CO 80220
CONNECTICUT	Vital Records Department of Health Services 150 Washington Street Hartford, CT 06106
DELAWARE	Office of Vital Statistics Division of Public Health P.O. Box 637 Dover, DE 19903

DISTRICT OF COLUMBIA

Vital Records Branch
Room 3009
425 I Street NW
Washington, DC 20001

FLORIDA

Dept. of Health and Rehabilitative Services
Office of Vital Statistics
1217 Pearl Street Jacksonville, FL 32202

GEORGIA

Georgia Department of Human Resources
Vital Records Unit
Room 217-H
47 Trinity Avenue SW
Atlanta, GA 30334

HAWAII

Office of Health Status Monitoring
State Department of Health
P.O. Box 3378
Honolulu, HI 96801

IDAHO

Vital Statistics Unit
Idaho Department of Health and Welfare
450 West State Street
Statehouse Mail
Boise, ID 83720-9990

ILLINOIS

Division of Vital Records
Illinois Department of Public Health
605 West Jefferson Street
Springfield, IL 62702-5079

INDIANA

Vital Records Section
State Board of Health
1330 West Michigan Street
P.O. Box 1964
Indianapolis, IN 46206-1964

IOWA	Iowa Department of Public Health Vital Records Section Lucas Office Building 321 East 12th Street Des Moines, IA 50319
KANSAS	Office of Vital Statistics State Dept. of Health and Environment 900 Jackson Street Topeka, KS 66612-1290
KENTUCKY	Office of Vital Statistics Department for Health Services 275 East Main Street Frankfort, KY 40621
LOUISIANA	Vital Records Registry Office of Public Health 325 Loyola Avenue New Orleans, LA 70112
MAINE	Office of Vital Records Human Services Building Station 11 State House Augusta, ME 04333
MARYLAND	Division of Vital Records Department of Health and Mental Hygiene Metro Executive Building 4201 Patterson Avenue P.O. Box 68760 Baltimore, MD 21215-0020
MASSACHUSETTS	Registry of Vital Records and Statistics 150 Tremont Street, Room B-3 Boston, MA 02111

Chapter X - Where to Write for Vital Records

MICHIGAN
Office of the State Registrar and
Center for Health Statistics
Michigan Department of Public Health
3423 North Logan Street
Lansing, MI 48909

MINNESOTA
Minnesota Department of Health
Section of Vital Statistics
717 Delaware Street, SE
P.O. Box 9441
Minneapolis, MN 55440

MISSISSIPPI
Vital Records
State Department of Health
2423 North State Street
Jackson, MS 39216

MISSOURI
Department of Health
Bureau of Vital Records
1730 East Elm
P.O. Box 570
Jefferson City, MO 65102

MONTANA
Bureau of Records and Statistics
State Dept of Health and Environmental Sciences
Helena, MT 59620

NEBRASKA
Bureau of Vital Statistics
State Department of Health
301 Centennial Mall South
P.O. Box 95007
Lincoln, NE 68509-5007

NEVADA
Division of Health-Vital Statistics
Capitol Complex
505 East King Street #102
Carson City, NV 89710

NEW HAMPSHIRE	Bureau of Vital Records Health and Human Services Building 6 Hazen Drive Concord, NH 03301
NEW JERSEY	State Department of Health Bureau of Vital Statistics South Warren and Market Streets CN370 Trenton, NY 08625
NEW MEXICO	Vital Statistics New Mexico Health Services Division 1190 St. Francis Drive Santa Fe, NM 87503
NEW YORK	Vital Records Section State Department of Health Empire State Plaza Tower Building Albany, NY 12237-0023
NEW YORK CITY	Bureau of Vital Records Department of Health of New York City 125 Worth Street New York, NY 10013
NORTH CAROLINA	Department of Environment, Health and Natural Resources Division of Epidemiology Vital Records Section 225 North McDowell Street P.O. Box 27687 Raleigh, NC 27611-7687

NORTH DAKOTA	Division of Vital Records State Capitol 600 East Boulevard Avenue Bismarck, ND 58505
OHIO	Division of Vital Statistics Ohio Department of Health G-20 Ohio Department Building 65 South Front Street Columbus, OH 43266-0333
OKLAHOMA	Vital Records Section State Department of Health 1000 Northeast 10th Street P.O. Box 53551 Oklahoma City, OK 73152
OREGON	Oregon Health Division Vital Statistics Section P.O. Box 116 Portland, OR 97207
PENNSYLVANIA	Division of Vital Records State Department of Health Central Building 101 South Mercer Street P.O. Box 1528 New Castle, PA 16103
SOUTH CAROLINA	Office of Vital Records and Public Health Statistics South Carolina Department of Health and Environmental Control 2600 Bull Street Columbia, SC 29201

SOUTH DAKOTA	State Department of Health Center for Health Policy and Statistics 523 East Capitol Pierre, SD 57501
TENNESSEE	Tennessee Vital Records Department of Health and Environment Cordell Hull Building Nashville, TN 37219-5402
TEXAS	Bureau of Vital Statistics Texas Department of Health 1100 West 49th Street Austin, TX 78756-3191
UTAH	Bureau of Vital Records Utah Department of Health 288 North 1460 West P.O. Box 16700 Salt Lake City, UT 84116-0700
VERMONT	Vermont Department of Health Vital Records Section Box 70 60 Main Street Burlington, VT 05402
VIRGINIA	Division of Vital Records State Health Department P.O. Box 1000 Richmond, VA 23208-1000
WASHINGTON	Vital Records 1112 South Quince P.O. Box 9709, ET-11 Olympia, WA 98504-9709

WEST VIRGINIA   Vital Registration Office
                         Division of Health
                         State Capitol Complex Building 3
                         Charleston, WV 25305

WISCONSIN   Vital Records
                         1 West Wilson Street
                         P.O. Box 309
                         Madison, WI 53701

WYOMING   Vital Records Services
                         Hathaway Building
                         Cheyenne, WY 83002

* U.S. Department of Health and Human Services
Public Health Service
National Center For Health Statistics
June 1990

CHAPTER XI - GENEALOGICAL RECORDS

The National Archives of the United States is a source of genealogical information. There are two locations of archives depositories: Washington, D.C. and St. Louis, MO.

The Federal records most frequently consulted for genealogical information are:

- Census Records
- Military Service and Pension Records

If you are searching for an ancestor who served in the U.S. military before WWI, you may request NATF Form 26, "Order for Copies of Veterans Records", from any regional archives branch or the:

>Reference Services Branch (NNIR)
>National Archives and Records Service
>Washington, D.C. 20408

For information about veterans who served during and after WWI, request Standard Form 180, "Request Pertaining to Military Records", available from any regional archives branch, the Reference Services Branch, or:

>National Personnel Records Center (MPR)
>9700 Page Boulevard
>St. Louis, MO 63132

Passenger Arrival and Naturalization Records

If you are searching for an ancestor who immigrated to the U.S. by ship to an eastern or gulf coast port between 1819 and 1940, you can request a search of the records in the National Archives Building in Washington, D.C. Your request should be submitted on NATF Form 40, "Order and Billing for Copies of Passenger Arrival Records", available from any regional archives branch or:

>Reference Services Branch (NNIR)
>National Archives and Records Service
>Washington, DC 20408.

Virtually no passenger lists exist for the pre-1820 period because the Federal Government did not require their submission at ports of entry. Lists compiled after the 1940's are maintained by the Immigration and Naturalization Service.

Microfilm copies of some passenger arrival records for specific areas served are located at some of the regional archives branches.

Land Records

If you are searching for an ancestor who acquired land directly from the Federal Government in a public land state you can request a search of the national archives in the Washington, D.C. area. There is no form to fill out, simply furnish a letter with:

- your ancestor's full name
- the name of the state in which he or she acquired land whether acquisition was before or after 1908
- any additional information you have about the land to:

> General Branch (NNFG)
> National Archives and Records Service
> Washington, DC 20409

Other records may be available depending on the type of contact the person may have had with the Federal Government, and how that contact may have created a record. Even some Indian tribes are recorded when the Federal Government moved the tribes west. There are no Federal census records before 1790. Census records for each decade after 1910 are not open for research until 72 years after the date they were created. (1920 Census opened in 1992)

GENEALOGICAL RESEARCH

Finding your ancestors and making a family tree for future generations may be up to you. The National Archives Library staff does not do family research, however there are professional searchers available.

Start with whatever information you may know about yourself and your family and you are ready to begin a genealogy search for the unknown.

Searching should begin at home with any information you may have in family Bibles, newspaper clippings, military certificates, birth and death certificates, diaries, letters, scrapbooks, and babybooks.

Organize whatever information you may have such as names, dates, places and relationships. These are the keys of the family searcher. People can be identified in records by their names, the dates of events (birth, marriage, death), by places where they resided, and by their relationships to others.

Write, call or visit relatives (particularly older relatives) and collect whatever information each person may provide. You may want to print a "Family Questionnaire" and conduct a "Survey". You may even want to advertise in a genealogical magazine, usually available in public libraries or bookstores.

Since birth and death registration became a requirement around the turn of the century (1890-1915) the only records that existed prior to this time period were those recorded in churches and family Bibles. When counties became established, records of marriages were started. Records of property acquisition and disposition are good sources of genealogical research. Such records are kept in county courthouses and often transferred to either a local or state archives library. Older records are microfilmed and can usually be accessed at a state archives library. Also available at state archives libraries are military records of all persons who enlisted and were discharged from that state. Libraries, historical and genealogical societies, and archival depositories are all good sources for genealogical and family history data. Many good books are available on how to do genealogical research. Several computer bulletin boards are currently available for searchers. U.F.O. has such a bulletin board for anyone searching for a relative. For more information write:

    MPB
    P.O. Box 290333
    Nashville, TN 37229-0333

The National Archives has millions of records relating to persons who have had dealings with the federal government. The records most useful for genealogical research are briefly described in this chapter. These records may contain full information about the person or give little information beyond a name. Searches in the records may be very time consuming as many records lack name indexes. The National Archives staff is unable to make extensive searches but, given enough identifying information, the staff will attempt to find a record about a specific person.

Most of the records, subject to the restrictions and limitations described below, may be freely consulted at the National Archives in Washington, DC or the General Branch, Civil Archives Division, in Suitland, MD. Photo copies of most of the records can be supplied for a moderate fee per page. If you are unable to come to the National Archives, you may hire someone to research for you. Many researchers who work for a fee advertise in genealogical periodicals, which are usually available in public libraries. A more detailed description of records of genealogical interest is contained in Guide to Genealogical Research in the National Archives.

CENSUS RECORDS

A census of the population has been taken every 10 years since 1790. The National Archives has the 1790-1870 schedules, a microfilm copy of the 1880 schedules, the surviving fragments of the 1890 schedules, and a microfilm copy of the 1900 and 1910 schedules. Practically all of the 1890 census schedules were destroyed by fire in 1921. The remaining entries are for small segments of the populations of Perry County, AL, the District of Columbia, Columbus, GA, Mound Township, IL, Rockford, MN, Jersey City, NJ, Eastchester and Brookhaven Township, NY, Cleveland and Gaston Counties, NC, Cincinnati and Wayne Township, OH, Jefferson Township, SD, and Ellis, Hood, Kaufman, Rusk, and Trinity Counties, TX.

The 1790-1840 schedules give the names of the head of household only; other family members are tallied unnamed by age and sex. For the 1850 and 1860 censuses, separate schedules list slave owners and the age, sex, and color (but not the name) of each slave. The 1850 and 1860 schedules include the name, age, and state, territory, or country of birth of each free person in a household. Additional information is included with each succeeding census.

The available schedules for the 1790 census were published by the federal government in the early 1900s and have since been privately reprinted. The published census schedules for 1790 are for Connecticut, Maine, Maryland, Massachusetts, New Hampshire, New York, North Carolina, and Vermont. Schedules for each state are listed in a separate, indexed volume. The schedules for the remaining states; Delaware, Georgia, Kentucky, New Jersey, Tennessee and Virginia, were burned during the War of 1812. As a substitute for the Virginia schedules, the federal government published names obtained from state censuses and tax lists, thereby listing about half of the known population of the state in 1790. Over the years additional lists of names have been published privately, and they provide more of the missing information for Virginia and other states whose 1790 schedules were destroyed. The government has not published other census listings, but many privately published lists are available from libraries and other sources. Although the lists vary considerably in format and geographic scope, they frequently save researchers from fruitless searches and help locate a specific entry in the actual records.

Also helpful in locating specific census entries are the following unpublished indexes in the National Archives Building:

- 1810 Census - a card index for Virginia only.
- 1880 Census - a microfilm copy of a card index to entries for each household that included a child aged 10 or under. On the cards are the name, age, and birthplace of each member of such households, and there is a separate cross-reference card for each child aged 10 or under whose surname is different from that of the head of the

household in which he is listed. The cards are arranged by state and thereunder by the Soundex system; that is alphabetically by the first letter of the surname, thereunder by the sound of the surname, and thereunder alphabetically by the given name of the head of the household.

- 1890 Census - a card index to the 6,160 names on the surviving 1890 schedules.
- 1900 Census - a microfilm copy of a card index to all heads of families. Otherwise, content is similar to 1880 index. * 1910 Census - a microfilm copy of an index to all heads of families in the following states: Alabama, Arkansas, California, Florida, Georgia, Illinois, Kansas, Kentucky, Louisiana, Michigan, Mississippi, Missouri, North Carolina, Ohio, Oklahoma, Pennsylvania, South Carolina, Tennessee, Texas, Virginia, and West Virginia. Content of the index is similar to the 1880 index.

OTHER CENSUSES

The National Archives has the 1890 special schedules of Union veterans and widows of veterans for Washington, DC. about half of Kentucky, and for states in alphabetical order from Louisiana through Wyoming. Schedules for the other states no longer exist. The schedules give the name and post office address of each living veteran and of each veteran's widow (along with the name of her deceased husband) and information about the service of each veteran named.

MICROFILM

The National Archives has microfilmed all of the available census schedules and the indexes to them, and positive microfilm copies are available at a moderate cost per roll. These microfilm rolls are arranged alphabetically by state and thereunder alphabetically by county. Usually all of the schedules for one county are on the same roll; some rolls contain records for several counties. The National Archives publications Federal Population Censuses, 1790-1890, 1900 Federal Population Census, and 1910 Federal Population Census, contain roll listings. These publications may be purchased for $2 each at the National Archives or may be ordered by sending a check or money order, payable to the National Archives Trust Fund Board, to the Publications Sales Branch (NEPS), Dept. 506, National Archives, Washington, DC 20408. Be sure to specify exact title(s) being ordered. Microfilm copies of census schedules 1790-1910 are available in the National Archives field branches and are available for use in the branches' research rooms.

MORTALITY SCHEDULES

The National Archives acquires microfilm copies of the mortality schedules of the 1850-80 censuses from the various depositories where they are held, whenever possible. For each person who died during the year that preceded the taking of each of the censuses, the schedules show the name, the month and the cause of death, and the state, territory, or country of birth. The National Archives has some or all of the available mortality schedules on microfilm for the following states: Arizona, Colorado, District of Columbia, Delaware, Georgia, Illinois, Kansas, Kentucky, Louisiana, Massachusetts, Minnesota, Montana, Nebraska, New Jersey, North Carolina, North Dakota, South Carolina, Tennessee, Texas, Utah, Vermont, Virginia, and Washington. Mortality schedules for other states are available in state archives, libraries, historical societies, and university libraries.

DISTRICT OF COLUMBIA RESIDENTS

Records relating to District of Columbia residents in the General Branch, Civil Archives Division, Suitland, MD, include, in addition to naturalization records, copies of wills, 1801-88; records relating to the administration of estates, 1801-78; and guardianship papers, 1802-78. Although the records relating to the administration of estates are concerned mostly with financial transactions involving the property and debts of a decedent, they show the personal name and sometimes names of family members. Copies of wills contain, besides the name of the decedent, the names of legatees and their relationship to the decedent. Guardianship papers give the name of each ward of the court and, at times, age and the names of parents. A search of these records requires the name of the person in question, the type of record involved, and the approximate date of the transaction.

INDIANS

There are in the National Archives many records relating to Indians who kept their tribal status. Most of the records, arranged by tribe, are dated 1830-1940. They include the following:

- List of Indians (chiefly Cherokee, Chickasaw, Choctaw, and Creek) who moved west during the 1830-46 period. Each entry on these lists usually contains the name of the head of the family, the number of persons in the family by age and sex, a description of property owned before removal (including the location of real property), and the dates of departure from the East and arrival in the West.
- Annuity payrolls, 1841-1949. Except for the early ones that give little but the names of heads of families, these show name, age, and sex of each person who received payment.
- Annual census rolls, 1885-1940 (available on microfilm), which normally show for each person in a family the Indian or English name (or both names), age, sex, and relationship to the head of the family and sometimes to another enrolled Indian. Occasionally on the rolls may be found supplementary information, such as names of persons who died or were born during the year. The National Archives staff will search the records if given the Indian's name (preferable both English and Indian names), the tribe, and the approximate date of association with the tribe.
- The Eastern Cherokee claim files, 1902-10, usually contain for each applicant the name, residence, date and place of birth, name and age of spouse, names of father and mother and children, and other genealogical information. For a search of the claim files, the name or claim number of claimant, age when the claim was filed, name of spouse, and names of parents or children will facilitate the search.

LAND RECORDS

The land records (dated chiefly 1800-1974) in the General Branch, Civil Archives Division, include bounty-land-warrant files, donation land entry files, homestead application files, and private land claim files relating to the entry of individual settlers on land in the public land states. There are no land records for the original 13 states and Maine, Vermont, West Virginia, Kentucky, Tennessee, Texas, and Hawaii. Records for these states are maintained by state officials, usually in the state capital. The donation land entry files and homestead application files show, in addition to the name of the applicant, the location of the land and the date it was acquired, residence or post office address, age or date and place of birth, marital status, and, if applicable, the given name of spouse or the size of family. If any applicant for homestead land was of foreign birth, the application file contains evidence of naturalization or of intention to become a citizen. Supporting documents show the immigrant's country of birth and sometimes the date and port of arrival. Genealogical information in records relating to private land claims varies from the mention of the claimant's name and location of the land to such additional information as the claimant's place of residence when the claim was made and the names of relatives, both living and dead.

The General Branch, Civil Archives Division, has a name index to land entries in Alabama, Alaska, Arizona, Florida, Louisiana, Nevada, and Utah for the period 1800-July 1, 1908, and for land entries after 1908 in the public land states. The staff will search the index if the full name of the applicant and the name of the state or territory in which the land was located are given. A search of the records for all other public land states or territories, 1800-1908, requires, in addition to the applicant's name, (1) a description of the land by township, range, section, and fraction of section or (2) the name of the land office, type of entry, and certificate number. An inquirer may be able to obtain the legal description of land by writing to the county recorder of deeds in the county seat of the county in which the land was located.

NATURALIZATION RECORDS

The General Branch, Civil Archives Division, has naturalization proceedings of the District of Columbia courts, 1802, 1926. These records show, for each person who petitioned for naturalization, name, age or date of birth, nationality, and whether citizenship was granted. The staff will search these records for information about naturalization that occurred before September 27, 1906, if given the full name of the petitioner and the approximate date of naturalization. Persons who wish information about citizenship granted elsewhere before September 27, 1906, should send their inquiries to the clerk of the federal, state, or other court that issued the naturalization certificate. The Immigration and Naturalization Service, Washington, DC 20536, has duplicate records of all naturalization that occurred after September 26, 1906. Inquiries about citizenship granted after that date should be sent to the Service on a form that can be obtained from any of the Service's district offices. Local postmasters will give the address of the nearest district office.

PASSENGER LISTS

The National Archives has several incomplete series of customs passenger lists and immigration passenger lists of ships arriving from abroad at many Atlantic, Pacific, and gulf coast ports. There are also arrival records for immigration via Canada. Customs passenger lists begin in 1820 and extend to the late 19th century (1890's) for most ports. The immigration passenger lists begin at that time, usually when the customs lists leave off.

PORT	PASSENGER ARRIVAL LISTS	INDEXES/YEAR
Baltimore	1820-1948	1820-1952
Boston	1820-1874	1848-1891
	1883-1943	1902-1920
New Orleans	1820-1945	1853-1952
New York	1820-1954	1820-1946
		1897-1948
Philadelphia	1800-1945	1800-1948
San Francisco	1893-1953	1893-1934
Seattle	1890-1957	
Arrivals via Canada	1895-1954	1895-1952
Certain minor ports	1820-1873	1890-1924
	1893-1954	

Chapter XI - Genealogical Records

Supplementing the indexes listed above is a general index to quarterly reports of arrivals at most ports except New York, 1820-74. Passenger lists before 1820 are not in the National Archives except for a small, incomplete collection for the port of Philadelphia. They may be on file at the port of entry or in the state archives where the port is located. Passenger and Immigration List Index: A Guide to Published Arrival Records..., by P. William Filby, and A Bibliography of Ship Passenger Lists, 1583-1825, by Harold Lancour, are guides to published lists of early immigrants to North America. Your local library may either have these publications or be able to assist you in locating copies.

A customs passenger list normally contains the following information for each passenger: name, age, sex, and occupation; the country of embarkation; and the country of destination. For one who died in passage, the date and circumstances of death are given. Immigration passenger lists vary in informational content but usually show the place of birth and last place of residence in addition to the information found in the customs passenger lists. Some of the immigration passenger lists include the name and address of a relative in the country from which the passenger came.

National Archives staff will search the customs passenger lists if in addition to the names of the passenger and the port of entry an inquirer can supply the following information: the name of the vessel and the month and year of its arrival or the name of the port of embarkation and the exact date of arrival. It will also search the immigration passenger lists up to 1954 when the lists are held by the National Archives if an inquirer can give the full names and ages of the passenger and of accompanying passengers, the port of entry, the vessel, and exact date of arrival. The staff will also consult existing indexes to the names on the customs and immigration passenger lists provided an inquirer can supply the name of the port of entry and month and year of arrival. Requests for searches should be made on NATF Form 81, Order and Billing for Copies of Passenger Lists. Microfilm copies of available passenger lists earlier than 1955 can be used in the National Archives.

The Morton Allen Directory of European Passenger Steamship Arrivals (New York, 1931) lists by year, steamship company, and exact date the names of the vessels arriving at the ports of New York, 1890-1930, and Baltimore, Boston, and Philadelphia, 1903-26. This publication is available in some large public and research libraries.

PASSPORT APPLICATION

The National Archives has passport applications and related papers, 1791-1926, of U.S. citizens who intended to travel abroad. The staff will make limited searches for age and citizenship information in these records that are at least 75 years old. The name of the person who applied for a passport and the place and approximate date of application should be supplied. Requests for information from passport records after 1926 should be addressed to the Passport Office, Department of State, Washington, DC 20520.

PERSONNEL RECORDS

There are a few records in the National Archives relating to civilian employees of the federal government whose service ended before 1910. These records may contain information about the date and place of birth of an employee. The National Archives staff will search for records about employees if given the full name and address of the employing agency and the approximate dates of employment. The personnel records for most civilian employees whose service terminated after 1909 are in Civilian Personnel Records, 111 Winnebago Street, St. Louis, MO 63118.

CLAIMS FOR PENSIONS AND BOUNTY LAND

Under numerous laws passed since the Revolutionary War period, money and land have been awarded to U.S. Army, Navy, and Marine veterans and their widows and other dependents. Each claim-whether for bounty land or pensions, whether submitted by the veteran or a relative, or whether or not approved-is filed under the name of the veteran on whose service the claim is based. The National Archives has bounty-land-warrant application files based on service in wartime between 1775 and 1855 and pension application files based on service between 1775 and 1916. Pensions based on military service for the Confederate States of America were authorized by some southern states but not by the federal government until 1959. Inquiries about state pensions should be addressed to the state archives or equivalent agency at the capital of the veteran's state of residence after the war.

Because the form and contents of papers submitted in support of claims have varied over the years, the information in the files is not uniform. A veteran's claim will probably show his place and date of birth, place of residence after service, and a summary of military service. A dependent's claim normally includes the dependent's age and residence, relationship to the veteran, and information about the veteran's death. A widow's application usually includes her maiden name, the date of her marriage to the veteran, and the names of their children.

Inquiries about pension and bounty-land claims should be submitted on NATF Form 80, Order and Billing for Copies of Veterans Records. Printed on the form are instructions for its use and an explanation of how orders are processed. When a claim file is found, documents that normally contain information of a personal nature about the veteran and his family will be selected and photocopied. The inquirer is notified of costs and copies are sent after payment is received. The selected documents furnished generally contain the basic information in the pension file, as the remaining documents rarely contain any additional genealogical data. If an inquirer wishes to have photocopies of all the reproducible papers in the claim file, they can be furnished for a moderate cost per page. The National Archives staff cannot undertake to read all the documents in the claim file or to answer questions about them.

Some of the information requested on the form will be found in Index of Revolutionary War Pension Applications, revised and published in 1966 by the National Genealogical Society; in Report From the Secretary of War...in Relation to Pension Establishment of the United States, published in three volumes in 1835 as Senate Document 514, 23RD Congress, 1st session; and in List of Pensioners on the Roll January 1, 1933, published in five volumes in 1883 as Senate Executive

Document 84, 47th Congress, 2ND session. These publications are available in some large public and research libraries.

VITAL STATISTICS

The National Archives has records of births, marriages, and deaths at U.S. Army facilities. 1884-1912, with some records dated as late as 1928. The staff will search these records if provided with the following: birth records-name of child, names of parents, place of birth, and month and year of birth; marriage records - names of contracting parties; death records - name, date, place, and rank of deceased.

The National Archives also has some records of births and marriages of U.S. citizens abroad registered at Foreign Service posts. Birth and marriage records extend through 1941, and reports of some deaths extend through 1040. Requests for information about registrations made less than 75 years ago should be addressed to the Department of State, Washington, DC 20520. Requests for information about earlier registrations should be addressed to the Diplomatic Archives Branch (NNFD), National Archives, Washington, DC 20408.

For information about other original records of birth, marriage, and death, an inquirer should address the bureau of vital statistics, the church, or other appropriate local depository in the appropriate state, county, or city. To obtain a birth certificate, address the bureau of vital statistics in the capital city of the state in which the birth occurred, giving the date and place of birth. If there is no record of birth on file, the bureau will explain the procedure for filing a delayed birth certificate. The Superintendent of Documents, U.S. Government Printing Office, Washington, DC 20402, can supply the leaflet Where to Write for Vital Records: Births, Deaths, Marriages and Divorces.

- National Archives and Records Administration General Information Leaflet

For further genealogical help I recommend:

Everton's Genealogical Helper, a magazine dedicated to helping genealogists since 1947, Subscription is only $21.00. Call or write: The Everton Publishers, Inc., P.O. Box 368, Logan, UT 84321, 800-443-6325 or 801-752-6022.

Chapter XI - Genealogical Records

The Church of Jesus Christ of Latter-day Saints Library, Family History Department, 50 East North Temple Street, Salt Lake City, UT 84150, (801) 240-2399. Call or write for more information concerning contributing information to the Ancestral File or other information concerning the library and it's services. You don't have to be an experienced genealogical researcher to contribute your family information. If you need help gathering information, visit the Family History Library, family history centers or join a genealogical society.

The Church of Jesus Christ of Latter-day Saints in Salt Lake City, Utah began a main library in 1894 which has become the largest of its kind in the world. It has a collection of over one million rolls of microfilm, one hundred fifty thousand books, eight million Family Group Record forms, and many other records.

Most of the main library's records have been acquired through an extensive microfilming program started in 1938. Presently over 100 microfilmers are filming original documents in courthouses, churches and other archives throughout the world. The microfilmers send the rolls of film to Salt Lake City where they are preserved in a record vault in the nearby mountains. Microfilm copies can be ordered and sent to the branch libraries as well as ordered direct from the main library.

Genealogical research is a process of asking 5 basic questions:

1. What do I know about my family?
2. What do I want to learn about my family?
3. What records does the library have?
4. How do I obtain a record?
5. What do I do next?

Genealogical research is a process involving evaluating each new piece of information in order to determine what that information may lead to next. Working on a genealogy is like working a puzzle. Finding the missing pieces of the puzzle will lead to completing a finished picture. Finding information regarding relatives will complete the history of your family.

There are Regional Archives Branches located in:

ATLANTA
1557 St. Joseph Avenue
East Point, GA 30344
(404) 736-7477

BOSTON
380 Trapelo Road
Waltham, MA 02154
(617) 647-8100

CHICAGO
7358 South Pulaski Road
Chicago, IL 60629
(312) 581-7816

DENVER
Building 48, Denver Federal Center
Denver, CO 80225
(303) 234-5271

FORT WORTH
4900 Hemphill Street
P.O. Box 6216 (mailing address)
Fort Worth, TX 76115
(817) 344-5525

KANSAS CITY
2306 East Bannister Road
Kansas City, MO 64131

LOS ANGELES
24000 Avila Road Laguna
Niguel, CA 926771
(714) 831-4220

NEW YORK
Building 22-M O T Bayonne
Bayonne, NY 07002
(201) 823-7545

PHILADELPHIA
5000 Wissahickon Ave
Philadelphia, PA 19144
(215) 951-5591

SAN FRANCISCO
1000 Commodore Drive
San Bruno, CA 94066
(415) 876-9009

SEATTLE
6125 Sand Point Way NE
Seattle, WA 98115
(206) 422-4501

National Archives Publications of Genealogical Interest:

Genealogical Records in the National Archives, GIL 5(rev. 1977), 17 p.

Military Service Records in the National Archives of the U.S., GIL7(1974), 15 p.

Guide to Genealogical Research in the National Archives (1982), 304 p.

Federal Populations Censuses, 1970-1890: A Catalog of Microfilm Copies of the Schedules (1977), 90 p.

1900 Federal Population Census: A Catalog of Microfilm Copies of the Schedules (1978), 84 p.

The 1910 Federal Population Census: A Catalog of Microfilm Copies of the Schedules (1982), 44 p.

CHAPTER XII - LEGAL ADOPTION PROCESS

Each state has its own laws governing the adoption process. Only two states, Alabama and Kansas, have open adoption records. In order to search adoption records one must understand the adoption process for the state in which the search is being conducted. Knowledge of the laws for the years involved are beneficial so that the searcher may know exactly which court handled adoptions for that year and what requirements were in effect. Most legal adoptions leave a paper trail, from hospital records, to adoption agency records, to an attorney, to court records and finally to sealed records.

There are many exceptions to the adoption searches. For example an adoptee in search of a birth parent or other biological family member will search entirely different from a birth parent or other family member searching for an adoptee.

Some states may have a registry. It is advisable to check each state for current laws and procedures because these change frequently.

U.F.O. has a mutual-consent registry available (as well as a newsletter/magazine listing many active searches), not only for persons involved in adoption searches, but all persons searching for a missing loved one. This is a special computer database capable of matching anyone searching fora missing relative. An adoptee, birth parent, sibling or other member of a biological family may register and if both are registered the computer will automatically match them by the adoptee's date of birth. Non-adopted searches may be matched with various fields of information.

Special training seminars are offered upon request to train others how to search for themselves.

The average adoption searcher is not familiar with the adoption procedure, law or where to begin the search. Most adoption searchers waste both time and money because they do not know what they should do. Take the time to learn what is involved in the adoption process, then study the law that was in effect the year of the adoption as well as the current law. Laws change often and states vary, so there is no one rule to follow for every search. Even though states have "closed records", there is usually some way available to obtain information. Adoption searches are probably the most difficult of all searches — difficult, not impossible!

Most legal adoptions consist of the following "paper trail" steps:

1. Birth mother's medical records.
2. Birth mother chooses adoption placing agency.
3. Birth records at hospital.
4. Original birth certificate issued.
5. Birth mother signs a surrender date. (Birth mother may have 6 months to change her mind. Check law.)
6. Adoption agency places child either in a foster home or adoptive family.
7. Adoptive parents hire attorney.
8. Adoptive parents file a petition for adoption in a court of jurisdiction. (Usually not filed until surrender date is in effect. Check law.)
9. Adoption agency files follow-up paperwork with court. This may include: order of reference, interlocutory decree, or other required home studies.
10. Final adoption decree is issued (usually one year from the time the original petition is filed).
11. Amended birth certificate is issued with child's new name.
12. Adoption records are sealed. Depending on state law these records may not be opened without a court order.

Surrender date vary from year to year, state to state, jurisdiction to jurisdiction. The time may be two (2) weeks, six (6) months, or one (1) year).

ADOPTION RECORDS

Adoption laws vary in each state and jurisdiction, therefore each searcher is advised to first check the law of the state and jurisdiction before beginning the search. Laws change frequently so be sure to study the law for the year of the adoption as well as the current law.

At the time of writing this book only two states, Alaska and Kansas allow open access to adoption records by any member of the biological family. According to officials in these states the law has had positive results for all.

Many states allow adoptees to request non-identifying information at their age of majority. This information is just exactly what it says, non-identifying. There are no names whatsoever. The information may or may not be accurate. It is not unusual for adoptees to be furnished incorrect and inaccurate information to deliberately keep them from locating the biological family.

In certain states, adoptees are allowed to request identifying information at their age of majority (18, 19, 20, 21). Upon request for identifying information the state may conduct a search for biological families to obtain consent before releasing any information. In some states if the biological family cannot be located the adoptee may obtain a copy of their original birth certificate.

Biological families usually do not have any rights to ask for information concerning an adoptee. However, it is not unusual for a state to allow a member of a biological family to write a letter to the adoptee so that if the adoptee makes a request for identifying information the letter may be given to the adoptee upon request. This is merely a courtesy not a mandatory law.

It is recommended that members of biological families attempt to write the state and request that the letter be given to the adoptee upon request. This letter may be called a "Waiver of Confidentiality", releasing the state from a prior commitment to confidentiality.

It is further recommended that all persons searching for an adoptee or member of the biological family register in the Missing Persons Bureau mutual-consent registry. This registry will automatically match two persons who are searching for each other. To register in the mutual-consent registry send a self-addressed stamped envelope to request a MPB questionnaire. There is a $10.00 registration fee. A quarterly "SEARCHING" newsletter/magazine publishes hundreds of active searchers waiting to be reunited. Subscription rate for the newsletter/magazine is $20.00 per year. Send check or money order made to **U.F.O., Inc.** to:

>MPB/SEARCHING
>P.O. Box 290333
>Nashville, TN 37229-0333

ADOPTEE'S SEARCH FOR BIRTHPARENTS, SIBLINGS AND OTHER MEMBERS OF THE BIOLOGICAL FAMILY

According to Today's Child, it is absolutely vital to human development for an adoptee to know the truth about their identity. After months of research in the Vanderbilt Medical Library in Nashville, Tennessee, I became convinced of this need. Study after study was documented proving the need for this information. I realize that adoptees have a need that most of society misunderstands.

Traditionally there have been many myths associated with adoption. One of these myths is that an adoptee needs someone else to make all decisions of what is in their best interest. This is a most absurd belief. Unfortunately this belief not only controls the adoptee as a child, but also as an adult. No one knows better than an adoptee what is in their best interest. No one knows better than an adoptee what it is like to live with the "Unknown". No one knows better than an adoptee what it is like to have your rights denied. An adoptee should be allowed to make decisions of what is in their best interest. Adoptees need to know the truth about their identity.

Only two states, Alabama and Kansas, have open adoption laws. Most of the other states are closed records. Pleas for opening records fall on deaf ears. In most states a court order is required for an adoptee to see what is in the closed or sealed adoption record. A court order may only be issued in life and death situations or for a serious medical emergency. An adoptee must pay an attorney and court costs in addition to the cost of copies of the records. Adoptees are actually victims.

Adoptees who want to find answers about their medical history, their heredity or their biological families must wait until they are of age, usually 18 - 21 years of age before most states will allow them to ask for identifying information. Some states will give non-identifying information at age 18 and make the adoptee wait until 21 to request identifying information. After making a written request to the state, an adoptee must wait. The state may or may not search for the birthparents to obtain consent before releasing any information. Some states will allow a birthparent to write the adoptee a letter. The state will hold the letter until the adoptee asks for it. Upon written request from an adoptee, many states will give the adoptee this letter.

Some states charge a fee for searching for the birthparents. Some states have a registry. Each state has a different law. In most states, birthparents have no rights, but adoptees have some rights. Because the laws are different and change often, before you begin a search, become familiar with the current adoption law as well as the adoption law in the year of your birth. The law 20 or more years ago may have been completely different than it is now.

Before you begin a search there are a few things you must understand. The legal adoption process is not the only way a child is adopted. Some adoptions are private, some through independent agencies, some handled through an attorney or doctor, some through a public agency. Babies are even left on doorsteps or in church buildings. Babies are stolen. Mothers are tricked into signing papers they do not understand. The word adoption is actually a legal process. Unless a baby is adopted through a court system, the child may not actually be an adoptee. The child could be a foster child. Foster children are different from adopted children in that the legal process provides that an adopted child is entitled to the same privileges as a child born naturally to an adoptive family. The child has inheritance rights. A foster child may be in a temporary or permanent home. The parents may be paid by the state, an agency, or other source to take care of the child. The child may not have it's name changed or be entitled to inherit from this family. The foster child and the adopted child have different rights.

The legal adoption process may be different in each state so allow for the differences in the examples you are about to read. Understand that court systems and laws in each state are individual. Understand that the courts in various jurisdictions may go by different names such as Circuit, Probate, Chancery or even County. Usually only one or two courts within a county will be responsible for all adoptions. Determine which court clerk's office is responsible for keeping the records of what transpires in that particular court.

The clerk's office is the keeper of the books and is responsible for indexing all court appearances. Therefore all court appearances are logged in an index book (similar to keeping a diary). This book contains each person who appears in court, the reason for the appearance, the date, the attorney representing this person, the costs of appearing and references to minute books which tell even more about the court appearance.

Do not confuse these records with the sealed adoption records. Before there can be sealed records certain processes must take place. The Birth mother must sign a "Surrender" which terminates her rights to the baby. If a father is named, he must also sign a "Surrender". Each state, each time period may be different, but certain basic steps usually occur. The "Surrender" is only one step of the legal adoption process. The "Surrender" allows a birthparent a certain period of time in which to change their mind and not allow the child to be adopted. You must determine what this time period is for the year of your birth. Usually the time period for the birthparent to change their mind is less than 6 months. I have seen some as long as 1 year and some only 14 days.

Before beginning a search for your biological family, I suggest you do several things:

- Understand the adoption process. Read the laws at your local public library or state archives library. If you do not live near where you were born, call or write and request a reference librarian to make you a copy.
- Make a checklist of information you already know about yourself, such as your date of birth, the city and state of birth, the county of birth, the hospital, etc. The more information you have to start with the easier the search

Chapter XII - Legal Adoption Process

should be. It is absolutely necessary for you to obtain the name(s) of your birthparent(s).

- Write to the state office for adoptions in the state in which you were born and request your identifying information. State that you waive your rights to confidentiality in order to allow a member of your biological family to contact you if they are searching for you. Keep your address updated if you move. Even though this may not produce any results, it is a good idea to try.

- If you know the hospital in which you were born, you may request copies of your birth records with a medical authorization form which is merely a written request with your signature. (If you do not know your name at birth, the hospital will probably not give you anything, however if you know your name, they will probably give you both yours and your mother's records.

- You must keep all requests for information very simple and to the point. Do not even try to explain anything to anyone. This will only keep you from obtaining anything. The less said, the better.

- You will learn the "A" word (adoption) is a no-no. You must learn to ask questions as if you were working on your family tree — nothing more.

- If your adoptive parents have copies of your adoption and are understanding enough to share this information, you are on your way. If you do not have the adoption petition or final decree, this is what you must locate at a county court clerk's office.

- Adoptive parents are given an amended birth certificate when they adopt a baby. This information usually only contains the name of the adoptive parents and the new name of the baby. Seldom will there even be a hospital. Having copies of your adoption petition and final decree may reveal a placing agency. This is the information you need.

- If you were adopted through a private agency, this agency may have a copy of your records in storage. The same information contained in the sealed records may be in the agency's records. Remember, the birthparents selected the agency of their choice to handle the adoption, therefore this agency has lots of information. The majority of adoptions occur through a state office.

- After you have requested the identifying information from the state, located an amended or original birth certificate, determined the court of jurisdiction and the city and state in which your adoption took place, read the laws, obtained a copy of your adoption petition and/or final decree, you are ready to begin searching. You must locate the name of your birthparents. If the court of jurisdiction has a clerk's office with public records, ask to see the Docket Appearance Book, Index Book for Adoptions, or whatever name they may call it. You must ask for this book for the year of your birth. On rare occasions, the name of the birthparents may appear, or even the child's name prior to adoption.

- Older records may be on microfilm in an archives library. Many older records provide more identifying information. Once you locate the clerk's office and know what book to ask for, begin your search by looking for the names of the adoptive parents. Some entries may identify the name of the child. Many times these names may be adoptions by a family member, such as a stepfather adopting a step-child. Sometimes grandparents are appointed guardians.

- Not all records will pertain to your search, therefore, you must learn to eliminate certain records. You will learn to recognize which entries are family members only.

For additional information, write to:

U. F. O.
P.O. Box 290333
Nashville, TN 37229-0333

ALABAMA

STATE AGENCY

Alabama Department of Human Resources
64 North Union Street
Montgomery, AL

SUPPORT GROUPS

AGAPE
Rt. 1, Box 266-A
Fairhope, AL 36532

Alabama Friends of Adoption
Children's Aid Society
3600 8th Avenue South, #300
Birmingham, AL 35222

Dekalb County Families for Adoption
507 7th Street, NW
Ft. Payne, AL 35967

Winegrass Adoption Association
P.O. Box 6203
Dothan, AL 36302

CUB
Rt. 1, Box 210D
Geneva, AL 36340

ALASKA

STATE AGENCY

Alaska Department of Health and Social Services
Division of Family and Youth Services
Pouch H-05
Juneau, AK 99811

SUPPORT GROUPS

Adoptees Liberation Movement of America
Northwest Regional Office
P.O. Box 372
Glennallen, AK 99588

CUB
7105 Shooreson Circle
Anchorage, AK 99504

ARIZONA

STATE AGENCY

Arizona Department of Economic Security
1400 West Washington, #940A
Phoenix, AZ 85007

SUPPORT GROUPS

Flagstaff Adoption Search & Support
P.O. Box 1031
Flagstaff, AZ 86002

Search Triad
P.O. Box 1432
Litchfield Park, AZ 85340

Tracers, Ltd.
P.O. Box 18511
Tucson, AZ 85731

T.R.I.A.D.
P.O. Box 12806
Tucson, AZ 85732

ARKANSAS

STATE AGENCY

Arkansas Department of Human Services
P.O. Box 1437
Little Rock, AR 72203

SUPPORT GROUPS

Arkansas Adoption Triad
5900 Scenic Drive Little Rock, AR 72207

Searchline of Arkansas
Rt. 5, Box 29-B
Huntsville, AR 72740

CALIFORNIA

STATE AGENCY

California Department of Social Services
744 P Street, M.S 19-31
Sacramento, CA 95814

SUPPORT GROUPS

Adoptee Identity Discovery
P.O. Box 2159
Sunnyvale, CA 94087

Adoptees' Birthparents' Association
P.O. Box 33
Camarillo, CA 93011

Adoptees' Search Workshop
P.O. Box 039
Harbor City, CA 90710

Adoption Center of San Diego
5365 LaCuenta Drive
San Diego, CA 92124-1414

Adoption Council of Orange County
P.O. Box 10857
Costa Mesa, CA 92627

Adoption Reality
2180 Clover Street
Simi Valley, CA 93065

Adoption With Truth
P.O. Box 20276
Oakland, CA 94611

AMFOR - AMERICANS FOR OPEN RECORDS
P.O. Box 401
Palm Desert, CA 92261

Birth Family Research
2027 Finch Court
Simi Valley, CA 93063

Central Coast Adoption Support
94 Manchester Place
Goleta, CA 93117

Central Coast Adoption Support
1718 Longbranch Avenue
Grover City, CA 93433

Central Coast Adoption Support
1328 Charlotte Street
Santa Maria, CA 93454

Central Coast Adoption Support Group
P.O. Box 5165
Santa Maria, CA 93456

Christian Adoption and Family Service
2121 West Crescent Avenue, E
Anaheim, CA 92801

CUB
P.O. Box 1902
Studio City, CA 91604

CUB Branch
2041 Willowood Lane
Encinitas, CA 92027

CUB
10801 San Paco Circle
Fountain Valley, CA 92708

CUB
P.O. Box 3265
Quail Valley, CA 92380

CUB
8632 Coolwoods Drive
Sacramento, CA 95825

CUB
P.O. Box 3193
Santa Barbara, CA 93130

CUB, Riverside
10801 San Paco Circle
Fountain Valley, CA 92708

CUB, San Diego
2041 Willowood Lane
Encinitas, CA 92024

Family Search Services
P.O. Box 587
Camarillo, CA 93011

Independent Adoption Center
3333 Vincent Road, Ste. #222
Pleasant Hill, CA 94523

Independent Search Consultants
P.O. Box 10192
Costa Mesa, CA 92627

La Casa
P.O. Box 1902
Studio City, CA 91604

Mendo Lake Adoption Triad
P.O. Box 487
Hopland, CA 95449

PACER
Ygnacio Woods Building L
2255 Ygnacio Valley Boulevard
Walnut Creek, CA 94598

Parenting Resources
250 El Camino Real, Ste. #111
Tustin CA 92680

P.A.S.T.
P.O. Box 24095
San Jose, CA 95154

Professional Adoption Search Team
P.O. Box 24095
San Jose, CA 95154

Search Finders of California
P.O. Box 24595
San Jose, CA 95154

Triadoption Library
P.O. Box 638
Westminster, CA 92684

Truthseekers in California
1053 Filbert
San Francisco, CA 94133

COLORADO

STATE AGENCY

Colorado Dept. of Social Services
1575 Sherman Street
Denver, CO 80203-1714

SUPPORT GROUPS

Adoptees in Search
P.O. Box 323, Contract Stn. 27
Lakewood, CO 80215

Birthparents' Group
P.O. Box 16512
Colorado Springs, CO 80935

CUB
P.O. Box 22904
Denver, CO 80222

Lambs in Search Ministry
3578D Parkmoor Village
Colorado Springs, CO 80907

Orphan Voyage
2141 Road 2300
Cedaredge, CO 81413

Reunion
P.O. Box 112
Salinda, CO 81201

CONNECTICUT

STATE AGENCY

Connecticut Department of
Children and Youth Services
170 Sigourney Street
Hartford, CT 06105

SUPPORT GROUPS

Adoptees' Search Connection
1203 Hill Street
Suffield, CT 06078

CUB Branch
P.O. Box 558
Bethel, CT 06801

Family Life Center, Inc.
79 Birch Hill Road
Weston, CT 06883

Ties That Bind
P.O. Box 3119
Milford, CT 06478

DELAWARE

STATE AGENCY

Delaware Department of
Children, Youth, and Their
Families
1824 Market Street
Wilmington, DE 19801

SUPPORT GROUPS

Lifeline International
702 Brandywine Boulevard
Wilmington, DE 19809

Trialog
2005 Baynard Boulevard
Wilmington, DE 19802

Tri-Love
P.O. Box 526
New Castle, DE 19720

DISTRICT OF COLUMBIA

STATE AGENCY

District of Columbia Department
of Human Services
500 1st Street N.W., 8th Fl.
Washington, DC 20001

SUPPORT GROUPS

Adoptee-Birthparent Support
Network L'Enfant Plaza Station
P.O. Box 44040
Washington, DC 20026-0040

American Adoption Congress
L'Enfant Plaza Station
P.O. Box 44040
Washington, DC 20026-0040

FLORIDA

STATE AGENCY

Florida Department of Health
and Rehabilitative Services
1317 Winewood, Building 8
Tallahassee, FL 32301

SUPPORT GROUPS

Adoption Triangle Ministry
P.O. Box 1860
Cape Coral, FL 33910

CARE
P.O. Box 714
Orange City, FL 32763

CUB
9008 University Boulevard
Orlando, FL 32817

CUB
552 Edward Rutledge Street
Orange Park, FL 32073

OASIS
P.O. Box 53-0761
Miami Shores, FL 33153

Oasis Chapter
P.O. Box 527
Dunedin, FL 33528

Oasis Chapter
P.O. Box 31512
St. Petersburg, FL 33732

Orphan Voyage of Florida
5360 Bridge Road
Cocoa, FL 32955

Orphan Voyage
13305 Southwest 100 Court
Miami, FL 33176

Chapter XII - Legal Adoption Process

Orphan Voyage
1120 N.E. 92nd Street
Miami Shores, FL 33138

Orphan Voyage
24409 Moss Creek Lane
Point Vedra, FL 32082

Orphan Voyage
1718 Palmer Lane
Rockledge, FL 32955

Orphan Voyage
13906 Pepperrell Drive
Tampa, FL 33624

Search Light, Inc.
1032 Vernonica Street
Port Charlotte, FL 33952

GEORGIA

STATE AGENCY

Georgia Department of Human Resources
878 Peachtree Street, N.E.
Atlanta, GA 30309

SUPPORT GROUPS

Caring Heart
P.O. Box 36111
Decatur, GA 30032

CUB
3374 Aztec Road 35C
Doraville, GA 30340

Roots and Wings
P.O. Box 32
Tucker, GA 30084

HAWAII

STATE AGENCY

Hawaii Department of Human Services
P.O. Box 339
Honolulu, HI 96809

SUPPORT GROUPS

None

IDAHO

STATE AGENCY

Idaho Department of Health and Welfare
Statehouse
Boise, ID 83720

SUPPORT GROUPS

Adopted Child
P.O. Box 9362
Moscow, ID 83843

CUB
P.O. Box 5202
Boise, ID 83705

ILLINOIS

STATE AGENCY

Illinois Department of Children and Family Services
100 West Randolph Street
Chicago, IL 60612

SUPPORT GROUPS

Adoption Triangle
P.O. Box 384
Park Forest, IL 60466

Hidden Birthright
3241 Saxony Road
Springfield, IL 62703

People Searching for People
1539 22nd Avenue
Rock Island, IL 61201

Truth Seekers in Adoption
P.O. Box 366
Prospect Heights, IL 60070

Yesterday's Children
P.O. Box 1554
Evanston, IL 60204

INDIANA

STATE AGENCY

Indiana Dept. of Public Welfare
Child Welfare/Social Services Division
131 South Meridian Street
Indianapolis, IN 46225

SUPPORT GROUPS

Adoptees' Family Circle
P.O. Box 1062
Richmond, IN 47374

Adoptee's Identity Doorway
P.O. Box 361
South Bend, IN 46624

Coping With Adoption
P.O. Box 1058
Peru, IN 46970

CUB
4501 Farnsworth
Indianapolis, IN 46241

Oasis Chapter
P.O. Box 3031
Kokomo, IN 46902

Reunion Registry of Indiana
P.O. Box 361
South Bend, IN 46624

Search for Tomorrow
P.O. Box 441
New Haven, IN 46774

Seek
213 Breamwold MS
Michigan City, IN 46360

Support of Search
P.O. Box 1292
Kokomo, IN 46901

IOWA

STATE AGENCY

Iowa Department of Human Services
Hoover State Office Building
Des Moines, IA 50319

SUPPORT GROUPS

Adoptees Quest
408 Buresh
Iowa City, IA 53340

Adoptive Experience Group
1105 Fremont
Des Moines, IA 50316

CUB National Headquarters
2000 Walker Street
Des Moines, IA 50317

CUB
500 Kimberly Lane
Des Moines, IA 50317

Iowa Reference and Reunion Library
Blairsburg, IA 50034

Orphan Voyage
P.O. Box 21
Cedar, IA 52543

KANSAS

STATE AGENCY

Kansas Department of Social and Rehabilitation Services
2700 West 6th Street
Topeka, KS 66606

SUPPORT GROUPS

Adoption Support Group
1425 New York Street
Lawrence, KS 66044

Reunions, Ltd.
2611 East 25th Street
Topeka, KS 66605

Wichita Adult Adoptees
5402 Polo
Wichita, KS 67208

KENTUCKY

STATE AGENCY

Kentucky Cabinet for Human Resources
275 East Main Street, 6th Floor West
Frankfort, KY 40621

SUPPORT GROUPS

Adoptees Awareness
P.O. Box 23019
Anchorage, KY 40223

A-Link
2159 Lansill Road
Lexington, KY 40504

CUB
P.O. Box 22795
Louisville, KY 40222

CUB
P.O. Box 13033
Lexington, KY 40583

Locators Unlimited
P.O. Box 1218
Nicholasville, KY 40340-1218

LOUISIANA

STATE AGENCY

Office of Human Development
Adoption Program
333 Laurel, Room 704
Baton Rouge, LA 70801

SUPPORT GROUPS

Adoptees' Birthright Committee
P.O. Box 7213
Metairie, LA 70010

Adoption Triad Network
P.O. Box 3932
Lafayette, LA 70502

Adoption Triad Network
P.O. Box 6175
Lake Charles, LA 70606

Adoption Triad Network
P.O. Box 1140
Morgan City, LA 70381

Adoption Triad Network
511 Blue Bell
Port Allen, LA 70605

Adoption Triad Network
P.O. Box 324
Swartz, LA 71281

Quebec Quest
814 North Lake Verret Court
Slidell, LA 70460

MAINE

STATE ADOPTION AGENCY

Department of Human Services 2
21 State Street
Augusta, ME 04333

SUPPORT GROUPS

Adoption Search Consultants, Maine
P.O. Box 793
South Portland, ME 04106

CUB
Rt. 1, Box 1017
West Paris, ME 04289

CUB
R.F.D. 2, Hilton's Lane
North Berwick, ME 03906

MARYLAND

STATE ADOPTION AGENCY

Department of Human
Resources
Social Services Administration
11 South Street
Baltimore, MD 32303

SUPPORT GROUPS

Adoptees in Search
P.O. Box 51016
Bethesda, MD 20014

Adoption Connection Exchange
1301 Park Avenue
Baltimore, MD 21217

MASSACHUSETTS

STATE ADOPTION AGENCY

Department of Social Services
150 Causeway Street
Boston, MA 02114

SUPPORT GROUPS

Adoption Connection, Inc.
O'Shea Building, #6
11 Peabody Square
Peabody, MA 01960

Boston Children's Service
Association
867 Boylston Street
Boston, MA 02116

Cape Association for Truth
P.O. Box 606
Woods Hole, MA 02543

Catholic Charitable Bureau of
Boston
10 Derne Street
Boston, MA 02114

CUB
P.O. Box 296, Harvard Square
Cambridge, MA 02138

The Family Center, Inc.
385 Highland Avenue
Somerville, MA 02144

New England Home for Little
Wanderers
161 Huntington Avenue
Jamaica Plain, MA 02136

Today Reunites Yesterday
P.O. Box 381
Easthampton, MA 01027

MICHIGAN

STATE ADOPTION AGENCY

Department of Social Services
P.O. Box 30037
Lansing, MI 48909

SUPPORT GROUPS

Adoptees Search for Knowledge
4227 South Belsay Road
Burton, MI 48519

Adoptees Search for Knowledge
P.O. Box 762
East Lansing, MI 48823

Adoption Identity Movement
13636 Podunk
Cedar Springs, MI 49319

Adoption Identity Movement
P.O. Box 9265
Grand Rapids, MI 49509

Adoption Identity Movement
P.O. Box 20092
Detroit, MI 48220

Adoption Insight
P.O. Box 153
Otsego, MI 49078

Adoption Triangle
4530 Lorenson Road
North Muskegon, MI 49445

Bonding by Blood Unlimited
4710 Cottrell Road, Rt. #5
Vassar, MI 48768

Catholic Social Services of
Washtenaw County
117 North Division
Ann Arbor, MI 48104

CUB
8017 Webster
Mt. Morris, MI 48458

Expectant Adoptive Parent
Classes
10602 Trailwood
Plymouth, MI 48170

Inheritance Research
P.O. Box 349
Calumet, MI 49913

Parent Finders
1602 Cole
Birmingham, MI 48008

Quebec Quest Reunion Registry
P.O. Box 4632
Union, MI 49130

Re-Traced Roots
P.O. Box 1390
Muskegon, MI 49443

Roots and Reunions
P.O. Box 121 L'Anse, MI 49946

Truth in the Adoption Triad
8107 Webster Road Mt. Morris,
MI 48458

MINNESOTA

STATE ADOPTION AGENCY

Department of Human Services
Human Services Building
444 Lafayette Road
St. Paul, MN 55155

SUPPORT GROUPS

CUB
4024 Quentin Avenue, South St.
Louis Park, MN 55416

LEAF
23247 Lofton Court, North
Scandia, MN 55073

MISSISSIPPI

STATE ADOPTION AGENCY

Mississippi Department of Public
Welfare
P.O. Box 352
Jackson, MS 39205

SUPPORT GROUPS

Independent Search Consultant
5108 Oak Meadow Avenue
Memphis, TN 38134

Independent Search Consultant
6536 Ferncrest
Memphis, TN 38134

MISSOURI

STATE ADOPTION AGENCY

Missouri Department of Social
Services
P.O. Box 88
Jefferson City, MO 65103

SUPPORT GROUPS

CARE
P.O. Box 30252 Plaza Stn.
Kansas City, MO 64112

Child Placement Services
201 West Lexington, Ste. #300
Independence, MO 84050

CUB
7000 Jackson
Kansas City, MO 64132

Kansas City Adult Adoptees
P.O. Box 15225 Kansas City, MO
64106

Searchline of Missouri
P.O. Box 274
Lampe, MO 65681

MONTANA

STATE AGENCY

Montana Department of Family
Services
P.O. Box 4210
Helena, MT 59604

SUPPORT GROUPS

Search
P.O. Box 181
Big Timer, MT 59011

NEBRASKA

STATE AGENCY

Nebraska Dept of Social Services
301 Centennial Mall, South
Lincoln, NE 68509

SUPPORT GROUPS

Midwest Adoption Triad
P.O. Box 37262
Omaha, NE 68137

NEVADA

STATE AGENCY

Dept. of Human Resources
Welfare Division
2527 North Carson Street
Carson City, NV 89710

SUPPORT GROUPS

Adoption Heritage
Search/Support
P.O. Box 85424
Las Vegas, NV 89185

NEW HAMPSHIRE

STATE AGENCY

New Hampshire Department of
Health and Human Services
6 Hazen Drive
Concord, NJ 03301

SUPPORT GROUPS

CUB
P.O. Box 64
Merrimack, NH 03054

NEW JERSEY

STATE AGENCY

New Jersey Division of Youth
and Family Services
1 South Montgomery Street
C.N. 719
Trenton, NJ 08625

SUPPORT GROUPS

Adoptive Parents for Open
Records
9 Marjorie Drive
Hackettstown, NJ 07840

CUB
58 West Franklin
Bound Brook, NJ 08805

Origins
P.O. Box 105
Oakhurst, NJ 07755

NEW MEXICO

STATE AGENCIES

New Mexico Human Services
Department
P.O. Box 2348
Santa Fe, NM 87504

SUPPORT GROUPS

Operation Identity
13101 Blackstone, N.E.
Albuquerque, NM 87111

NEW YORK

STATE AGENCY

New York State Department of
Social Services
40 North Pearl Street
Albany, NY 12243

SUPPORT GROUPS

Adopted People for Life
P.O. Box 321
Chappaqua, NY 10514

Adoptees' Information Service
19 Marion Avenue
Mt. Vernon, NY 10552

Adoption Circle
401 East 74th Street, Ste. #17D
New York, NY 10021

Adoption Friendship Circle
511 Winston Drive
Endwell, NY 13760

ALMA Society, Inc.
Washington Bridge
P.O. Box 154
New York, NY 10033

Birthparent Support Network
P.O. Box 120
North White Plaines, NY 10603

CUB
102 North Street
Manlius, NY 13104

Far Horizons
P.O. Box 621
Cortland, NY 13045

Northeast Adoption Association
1112 Parkwood Boulevard
Schenectady, NY 12308

The Right to Know
P.O. Box 52
Old Westbury, NY 11568

Rochester Adoption Coalition
P.O. Box 92181
Rochester, NY 14692

Searchline of New York
R.D. 2, Whitaker Road
Fulton, NY 13069

Society for Advancement of
Rights of Adoptees
P.O. Box 229
Syracuse, NY 13208

Suffolk Adoption Search and
Support
10 Janice Lane
Selden, NY 11022

NORTH CAROLINA

STATE AGENCY

North Carolina Department of
Human Resources
Division of Social Services
325 North Salisbury Street
Raleigh, NC 27611

SUPPORT GROUPS

Adoptees Together
P.O. Box 16532
Greensboro, NC 27406

Adoption Information Exchange
P.O. Box 4153
Chapel Hill, NC 27515

CUB
4916 Brentwood Road
Durham, NC 27713

NORTH DAKOTA

STATE AGENCY

North Dakota Department of Human Services
State Capitol-Judicial Wing
Bismarck, ND 58505

SUPPORT GROUPS

Independent Search Consultant
5402 Polo
Wichita, KS 67208

OHIO

STATE AGENCY

Ohio Department of Human Services
30 East Broad Street, 30th Floor
Columbus, OH 43215

SUPPORT GROUPS

Adoptees Search Rights
P.O. Box 132
Painesville, OH 44077

CUB
6557 Visitation Drive
Cincinnati, OH 45248

CUB
2544 Bonnie Lane
Maumee, OH 43537

CUB
5248 York Road, SW.
Patskala, OH 43062

CUB
5-561 Ann Avenue
Wauseon, OH 43567

Chosen Children
31 Springbrook Boulevard
Dayton, OH 45405

Reunite
P.O. Box 694
Reynoldsburg, OH 43068

Sunshine Reunion
1175 Virginia Avenue
Akron, OH 44306

T.R.A.C.E. II
P.O. Box 2414
Warren, OH 44484

OKLAHOMA

STATE AGENCY

Oklahoma Department of Human Services
P.O. Box 25352
Oklahoma City, OK 73125

SUPPORT GROUPS

Adoptees as Adults
1023 Arkansas
Norman, OK 74017

Adoptees as Adults
8220 Northwest 114th
Oklahoma City, OK 73132

Willows Graduates
R.R. 8, Box 324
Claremore, OK 74017

OREGON

STATE AGENCY

Oregon Department of Human Resources
Children's Services Division
198 Commercial Street, S.E.
Salem, OR 97310

SUPPORT GROUPS

Boys and Girls Aid Society of Oregon
2301 Northwest Glisan
Portland, OR 97210

Footprints
P.O. Box 764
Phoenix, OR 97535

The GS Foundation
9203 Southwest Cree Circle
Tualatin, OR 97062

Oregon Adoptees' Support Group
P.O. Box 12061
Salem, OR 97309

S.O.A.R.
P.O. Box 202
Grants Pass, OR 97526

S.O.A.R.
1076 Queens Branch Road
Rogue River, OR 97537

PENNSYLVANIA

STATE AGENCY

Pennsylvania Department of Public Welfare
Office of Children, Youth, and Families
P.O. Box 27653
Harrisburg, PA 17105

SUPPORT GROUPS

Adoption Forum
6808 Ridge Avenue (Rear)
Philadelphia, PA 19128

Adoption Lifeline of Altoona
414 28th Avenue
Altoona, PA 16601

CUB
P.O. Box 7673
Pittsburgh, PA 15021

CUB
2800 West Chestnut Avenue
Altoona, PA 16603

PAST
3847 Amidon Avenue
Erie, PA 16510

Pittsburgh Adoption Lifeline
P.O. Box 52
Gibsonia, PA 15044

RHODE ISLAND

STATE AGENCY

Rhode Island Department for Children and Their Families
610 Mt. Pleasant Avenue
Providence, RI 02908

SUPPORT GROUPS

Jewish Family Services
229 Waterman Street
Providence, RI 02906

PALM of Rhode Island
861 Mitchell's Lane
Middletown, RI 02840

SOUTH CAROLINA

STATE AGENCY

South Carolina Department of Social Services
P.O. Box 1520
Columbia, SC 29202-1520

SUPPORT GROUPS

Adoptees and Birthparents in Search
P.O. Box 6426B
Greenville, SC 29606

Adoptees and Birthparents in Search
P.O. Box 5551
West Columbia, SC 29171

Searchers of Lost Heritage
P.O. Box 29
Clemson, SC 29633

Triad, Inc.
P.O. Box 4778
Columbia, SC 29240

SOUTH DAKOTA

STATE AGENCY

South Dakota Department of
Social Services
Richard F. Kneip Building
700 Governor's Drive
Pierre, SD 57501

SUPPORT GROUPS

Independent Search Consultant
5402 Polo Wichita, KS 67208

TENNESSEE

STATE AGENCY

Tennessee Department of
Human Services
Citizens Plaza Building
400 Deaderick Street
Nashville, TN 37219

SUPPORT GROUPS

Adult Adoptees and
Birthparents in Search
P.O. Box 3572
Chattanooga, TN 37404

CUB
2601 Holston
Morristown, TN 37814

Independent Search and
Adoption Consultants
6536 Ferncrest
Memphis, TN 38134

Openness In Adoption
c/o Sandra Freeman
518 General George Patton Road
Nashville, TN 37221

ROOTS
P.O. Box 11522
Knoxville, TN 37939

Search Investigative Services
P.O. Box 9662
Knoxville, TN 37940

Society's Children
P.O. Box 527
Loudon, TN 37774

Tennessee Searchers for Truth
7721 White Creek Pike
Joelton, TN 37080

Tennessee's The Right To Know
P.O. Box 34334
Memphis, TN 38134

U.F.O., INC.
P.O. Box 290333
Nashville, TN 37229-033

*NATIONWIDE MUTUAL-CONSENT REGISTRY

M.P.B. (MISSING PERSONS
BUREAU)
U.F.O., INC.
P.O. Box 290333
Nashville, TN 37229-0333

TEXAS

STATE AGENCY

Texas Department of Human
Services
P.O. Box 2960
Austin, TX 78769

SUPPORT GROUPS

Adoption Awareness Center 6
15 Elm at McCullough
San Antonio, TX 78202

Adoption Counseling and
Consultation
6048 Hopes Ferry
San Antonio, TX 78233

Love, Roots and Wings
5039 Hacienda
San Antonio, TX 78233

Right to Know
P.O. 1409
Grand Prairie, TX 75051

Searchline of East Texas
2810 Judson Road, #1006
Longview, TX 75601

Searchline of Plano
3428 Garner
Plano, TX 75023

Searchline of Texas 3
313 Lombard
Amarillo, TX 79106

Searchline of Texas
Rt. 2, Box 2225B
Boerne, TX 78006

Searchline of Texas
1516 Old
Orchard Irving, Tx 75061

Searchline of Texas
5039 Hacienda
San Antonio, TX 78233

Triangle Search
5730 Crestgrove
Corpus Christi, TX 78415

UTAH

STATE AGENCY

Utah Dept. of Social Services
Office of Community Operations
Salt Lake Central Office
2835 South Main Street
Salt Lake City, UT 84115

SUPPORT GROUPS

Adoption Identity, Utah
P.O. Box 8124
Salt Lake City, UT 84108

CUB
5291 Cobble Creek Road, #25A
Salt Lake City, UT 84117

VERMONT

STATE AGENCY

Vermont Department of Social
and Rehabilitation Services
103 South Maine Street
Waterbury, VT 05676

SUPPORT GROUPS

CUB
R.D. 1, Box 716
Bridgeport, VT 05734

Friends in Adoption
P.O. Box 87
Pawlet, VT 05761

VIRGINIA

STATE AGENCY

Virginia Dept. of Social Services
8007 Discovery Drive
Richmond, VA 23229-8699

SUPPORT GROUPS

Adoptees and Natural Parents
5425 Willow Lake Road
Chesapeake, VA 23321

Alliance for Adoption Reform
P.O. Box 304
Springfield, VA 22150

Emancipation Consultants
Route 1, Box 251
Shawsville, VA 24162

WASHINGTON

STATE AGENCY

Washington Department of
Social and Health Services
Office Building #2
Olympia, WA 98504

SUPPORT GROUPS

ALMA Northwest Regional
Office
P.O. Box 372
Glennallen, AK 99588

Adoption Resource Center
Children's Home Society of
Washington
P.O. Box 15190
Seattle, WA 98115

Catholic Community Services,
Tacoma 5
410 North 44th
Tacoma, WA 98407

Children's Home Society of
Washington
P.O. Box 15190
Seattle, WA 98115

CUB
10014 Northeast 35th Street
Vancouver, WA 98662

Washington Adoptees' Rights
Movement
5960 6th Avenue, South, Ste.
#107
Seattle, WA 98108

WEST VIRGINIA

STATE AGENCY

West Virginia Department of
Human Services
1900 Washington Street, East
Charleston, WV 25305

SUPPORT GROUPS

Society's Triangle
411 Cabell Court
Huntington, WV 25703

WISCONSIN

STATE AGENCY

Wisconsin Department of Health
and Social Services
P.O. Box 7851
Madison, WI 53707-7851

SUPPORT GROUPS

Adoption Information and
Direction (AID)
P.O. Box 2152
Appleton, WI 54913

AID
P.O. Box 111
Cudahy, WI 53110

AID
P.O. Box 8162
Eau Claire, WI 54701

AID
P.O. Box 7371
Milwaukee, WI 53707-7371

AID
P.O. Box 23764 M
ilwaukee, WI 53224

AID
P.O. Box 2043
Oshkosh, WI 54903

AID
2117 Clark
Stevens Point, WI 54481

Common Bonds
1217 Indigo Drive
Oshkosh, WI 54901

CUB
2977 North Bartlett, #36
Milwaukee, WI 53211

WYOMING

STATE AGENCY

Wyoming Department of Health
and Social Services
Hathaway Building
Cheyenne, WY 82002-0710

SUPPORT GROUPS

Adoptive Parent Group
636 Bridger
Rock Springs, WY 82901

APPENDIX A
Sample Missing Person Profile

1. Name
    - A. Alias
    - B. Maiden
    - C. Adopted
2. Social Security Number
3. Drivers License Number and State
4. Age
5. Birth date
6. Last Known Address
7. All Other Addresses
8. Professional Designation
9. Military History
    - A. Rank and Branch
    - B. Assignments
10. Automobile - Boat - Motorcycle
    - A. License Number and State
    - B. VIN or Other Identification Number
    - C. Description
11. Associates
    - A. Relatives
    - B. Friends
    - C. Neighbors
    - D. Enemies

E. Clubs, Groups, Organizations, Associations
12. Marital Status
    A. Married, Divorced, Single, Widowed
    B. Ex-Spouse
    C. Children
    D. Alimony
    E. Child Support
    F. Other
13. Employment Status
    A. Businesses
    B. Corporations
    C. Taxes
    D. Licenses
    E. Skills/Special Training
    F. Employer
14. Medical Information
    A. Doctor
    B. Dentist
    C. Chiropractor
    D. Hospital
    E. Pharmacy
    F. Medical History
        1. Previous Illness
        2. Current or Known Medical Condition
    G. Medical Insurance/Claims
15.
    Assets

Appendix A - Sample Missing Person Profile

    A. Source of Income
    B. Property
    C. Vehicles
    D. Bank Accounts
    E. Other

16. Investments
    A. Stocks
    B. Bonds
    C. Retirement, Annuities
    D. Other

17. Insurance
    A. Life
    B. Medical
    C. Property
    D. Claims
    E. Worker's Compensation/Disability
    F. Dental
    G. Prescription

18. Debts
    A. Judgments/Liens
    B. Bankruptcy
    C. Mortgages
    D. Collections/Garnishments
    E. Loans

19. Characteristics
    A. Reputation

- B. Habits
- C. Hobbies
- D. Special Interests
- E. Recreation
20. Hang Outs
21. Other

APPENDIX B
Missing Person Motive Profile
(Reason for Leaving)

Foul play or voluntary?

Marital conditions?

Debts: financial condition?

Criminal involvement?

Medical problem?

Who will gain the most from the disappearance?

Patterns and lifestyle of the missing person.

Who is the missing person most likely to contact?

How will the missing person survive?

Why would this person not want to be located?

APPENDIX C
SAMPLE CRIMINAL HISTORY
RECORD CHECK REQUEST

FEES ARE DUE IN ADVANCE [CHOOSE TYPE(S) OF SEARCH]

1. Computer Search - FEE $5.00 - for years 1978 to present
2. Manual Search - Felony Convictions for years prior to 1978 (does not include computer search) - FEE $10.00 - Misdemeanor convictions prior to 1978 not available.

Receipt Number _____ Date _____

MAIL/DELIVER TO: Criminal Court Clerk
303 Metro Courthouse
Nashville, TN 37201

FROM:

_____
Authorized Signature

INFORMATION ON INDIVIDUAL TO BE RESEARCHED:

Full Name _____

Address _____

Sex   M   F   (Circle one)   Race

DATE OF BIRTH _____ Driver's License # _____

   NO RECORD LOCATED
(Initials of D. Clerk)

APPENDIX D
CHECKLIST FOR SEARCHERS

DIRECTORIES

☐ Telephone
☐ City

ASSEMBLE KNOWN INFORMATION

☐ Full Name
☐ Aliases Social Security Number
☐ Driver's License Number
☐ Hobbies and Habits
☐ Friends and Relatives
☐ Automobile License

COURT RECORDS

☐ Criminal
☐ Civil
☐ Traffic
☐ Probate
☐ Divorce
☐ Adoption
☐ Bankruptcy

COUNTY CLERK

☐ Automobile Registration
☐ Voter Registrar
☐ Tax Assessor
☐ Marriage License
☐ Property Tax
☐ Registrar of Deeds
☐ Occupational License

LAST KNOWN ADDRESS

☐ Landlord
☐ Neighbors
☐ Household Members
☐ Post Office
☐ Relatives
☐ Children
☐ Former Spouse

FINANCES

☐ Bank
☐ Credit Check
☐ Debtors
☐ Creditors
☐ Credit Card
☐ Stocks/Bonds/Investments

STATE

- ☐ Driver's License
- ☐ Driving History
- ☐ Accident Report
- ☐ Vehicle Registration
- ☐ Corporation Records
- ☐ Professional License
- ☐ Worker's Compensation Claims

OTHER

- ☐ Bankruptcy
- ☐ Military
- ☐ Internal Revenue Service
- ☐ Social Security Administration
- ☐ Schools
- ☐ Organizations
- ☐ Labor Unions
- ☐ Medical Records
- ☐ Insurance
  - » Medical
  - » Automobile
  - » Life
- ☐ Clubs
- ☐ Church

UTILITIES

- [ ] Gas
- [ ] Telephone
- [ ] Electric
- [ ] Water
- [ ] Newspaper
- [ ] Trash

APPENDIX E
MEDICAL AUTHORIZATION

Date_____(expires 6 months from this date unless indicated otherwise or revoked earlier).

Soley to assist_____, I hereby authorize any physician, hospital, pharmacy, dentist, employer or other person or organization possessing medical information concerning:

_____
_____

to permit the above named company or its representative(s) to view, copy, be furnished medical records: _____

_____
_____

MISSING PERSON QUESTIONNAIRE

©1992, U.F.O., Inc.

PLEASE TYPE OR PRINT CLEARLY.

SEARCHER INFORMATION:
1. Your Name: _____
2. Your Address: _____
   City: _____ ST ____ Zip: _____ Phone: ( ) _____
3. Date of birth: _____ Place of birth: _____
4. Social Security Number: _____ SEX: M F RACE: _____
5. Relationship to Missing Person: _____

MISSING PERSON INFORMATION
1. Missing Person's Full Name: _____
2. Last Known Address: _____
   City: _____ ST: _____ Zip: _____ Phone: ( ) _____
3. Age: _____ Date of Birth: _____ Place of Birth: _____
4. Social Security Number: _____ SEX: M F RACE: _____
5. Why is this person missing? _____
7. Please include other known information that may help locate this person: _____

ADOPTION INFORMATION

WHO IS THE ADOPTEE?   ☐ SEARCHER   ☐ MISSING PERSON

Adoptee's name at birth if known: _____
Birth Parent's name if known: _____

Agency: _____ Court: _____ City/State: _____

County: _____ Attorney: _____ Other: _____

Place of birth: Hospital: _____ City: _____ State: _____

Additional Information: _____

Payable by check, money order or credit card. Make payable to U.F.O., Inc.

Credit card #: _____ Exp. Date: _____

Signature: _____

Complete this form, and mail with **$10.00 REGISTRATION FEE** to:
MISSING PERSON REGISTRY
a DIVISION OF: U.F.O., Inc. / P.O. Box 290333 / Nashville, TN 37229-0333
(615) 366-5181   Fax: (615) 366-5481

AMERICA'S MOST WANTED LOVED-ONES

THE MISSING PERSON REGISTRY

ARE YOU SEARCHING FOR A MISSING LOVED-ONE?

HUNDREDS OF PEOPLE ARE WAITING TO BE REUNITED!

LET OUR COMPUTER MATCH YOU WITH YOUR LOVED-ONE.

ONLY $10.00
Free with purachase of book.

COMPLETE THE MISSING PERSON QUESTIONNAIRE INSIDE.

MISSING PERSON REGISTRY
P.O. BOX 290333
NASHVILLE, TN 37229-0333

NORMA TILLMAN

Private Investigator Norma Tillman has located over *1,000* missing persons. Her background includes 3 years with the Federal Government, 11 years with law-enforcement, 2 years of insurance fraud investigations and 6 years of private investigations. She is a Tennessee based investigator who has trained approximately *1200* other investigators through her seminars.

"I can honestly state that Norma Tillman's book is the most concise work of art I have ever read regarding the subject of locating anybody, anytime, anywhere. She has put down many, many years of actual street work and methods". John Wilson, Tech 2008 Newsletter. (22 year veteran P.I., Ret.)

ORDER FORM

☐ **BOOK: "SECRETS FOR SUCCESSFUL SEARCHING"** 39.95
   How To Find Almost Anyone

☐ **BOOK: "THE ADOPTION SEARCHER'S HANDBOOK"** 19.95
   A Guidebook for Adoptees, Birth Parents and Others involved in The Adoption Search.
   Anyone conducting an adoption search needs to understand the process before proceeding!

☐ **"MISSING PERSONS" MAGAZINE** (Quarterly Subscription) 20.00
   A Magazine To Help All Persons Who Are Searching For A Missing Relative or Friend.
   This magazine contains thousands of active searches of people waiting to be reunited.

☐ **NATIONWIDE MISSING PERSON COMPUTER REGISTRY** 10.00
   A computer that matches two persons searching for each other. Everyone must complete
   the missing person questionnaire and register in this computer! (Persons registered in this
   computer are selected for television reunions.)

☐ **SEMINAR:**
   "HOW TO FIND ALMOST ANYONE"
   (Please check box if you are interested in attending one of Norma's seminars.)

☐ **NATIONWIDE LOCATING SERVICES** 30.00 & up
   Computer information.
   (Surname searches; Social Security numbers traced; death records; address searches; etc.)

☐ **N.C.I. - NATIONAL CREDIT INFORMATION** 795.00
   The #1 source for information. (Certain restrictions apply- professionals only!)
   Free online demonstration: (513) 521-4420 - PASSWORD: DEMO53

☐ **VIDEO TAPES: -**
   "HOW TO FIND ALMOST ANYONE 59.95
   A professional training seminar taped during a live presentation by Norma Tillman. 1 hour 50 min.
   "THE ADOPTION PROCESS" 19.95

Name: _____
Address: _____
City/St/Zip: _____
Phone: _____
Method of Payment: Ck. ____ M/O ____ Amount Enclosed: _____
   Make payable to U.F.O., Inc.
Credit Card: VISA _____   MASTERCARD _____
Credit Card #: _____   Expiration Date: _____
Signature: _____

U.F.O., INC. / P. O. BOX 290333 / NASHVILLE, TN 37229-0333
(615) 366-5181 FAX: (615) 366-5481